Pan-Africanism
Caribbean Connections

Pan-Africanism Caribbean Connections

Ivor Agyeman-Duah
Abdul Karim Bangura
Mario D. Fenyo
Jim Perkinson

iUniverse, Inc.
New York Lincoln Shanghai

Pan-Africanism Caribbean Connections

iUniverse books may be ordered through booksellers or by contacting:

iUniverse
2021 Pine Lake Road, Suite 100
Lincoln, NE 68512
www.iuniverse.com
1-800-Authors (1-800-288-4677)

A publication of the African Studies and Research Forum, an affiliate of the Association of Third World Studies, under the auspices of The African Institution

ISBN: 978-0-595-45193-7 (pbk)
ISBN: 978-0-595-89501-4 (ebk)

Printed in the United States of America

† Nwafejoku Okolie Uwaclibie
A man who spent his life preparing future leaders in both Africa and the Diaspora

Contents

Acknowledgments

We, and hopefully many readers, owe gratitude to:

Mwalimu John Mukum Mbaku and Mwalimu Emanuel I. Udogu, for their leadership and support of this project.

Mwalimu Harold Isaacs, for his unflinching support of the work of the African Studies and Research Forum.

Mwalima Shanelle Wells, for providing impeccable copyediting, research and keyboarding assistance.

The numerous families to which we belong, for offering their encouragement and prayers.

Preface

Abdul Karim Bangura

This book is the result of essays presented on three panels of the same title at the 23rd Annual Meeting of the Association of Third World Studies (ATWS), which convened in Santo Domingo, Dominican Republic, September 20-22, 2005. The impetus for the panels and the subsequent book emerged from the desire to address the greatly neglected subject in academia of: the African legacy of Caribbean societies. We had hoped to go beyond an effort by a group of scholars who examined the same topic more than a quarter century ago (1979) in the book titled *Africa and the Caribbean: The Legacies of a Link,* edited by Margaret Grahan and Franklin W. Knight and published by Johns Hopkins University Press. Despite substantial financial and other support from several organizations, as the editors of the book lamented, their multidisciplinary effort yielded a relatively smaller number of contributions (seven chapters, a 159-page book). A similar fate befell our effort as well. With no financial or other support from any organization, a small number of us who had signed up to write and present essays on the subject attended the ATWS meeting in the Dominican Republic. We had developed panels that employ multidisciplinary approaches to examine issues dealing with the Pan-African principle, political and governmental connections, international organizational connections, legal (i.e. law) connections, economic connections, language and linguistic connections, intellectual and academic connections, literary connections, Creole cultural connections, religious and spiritual connections, musical connections, food and culinary connections, and arts and aesthetics connections. After two years of appealing to colleagues who had signed up for the project yielded no additional essays, we decided to proceed with the publication of this book so that our work does not become too dated. Despite this shortcoming, we hope that the six chapters in this book have added to and updated certain aspects that appear in the Grahan and Knight text.

The chapters that follow have, I believe, achieved two of the major goals we set for ourselves. The first goal is to show how literary works and practices have highlighted the relations between Africans in the continent and in the Diaspora and

1

interconnections among their social institutions. The primary subject matter is the societies—their patterns and arrangements, the processes through which they develop and change, and the interplay between these patterns and processes and the behavior of individuals and groups. The second goal is presenting the history of African cultures, their evolution and development, and their structure and functioning in the continent and in the Diaspora. The concern is with Africans' reactions in cultural forms to the ever-present problems posed by the physical environment, the attempts to live and work together, and the interactions between their various groups.

Evident in the chapters is the fact that the African life concept in the continent and in the Diaspora is holistic: that is, it is based on an integrative world view. All life to the African is total; all human activities are closely interrelated. This has as its underlying principle the sanctity of the person, his/her spirituality and essentiality. This essentialist view of the person confers value to his/her personhood. All else—his/her labor and achievement—flow from this value system. Even personal failure cannot invalidate it.

Also, for the African in the continent and in the Diaspora, politics defines duties and responsibilities alongside obligations and rights. All these relate to the various activities that have to do with survival. The survival concept is continuing, dynamic, and dialectical. The fundamental principle that is at the basis of this conception is one of morality.

Finally, the African moral order, whether in the continent or in the Diaspora, never defined rigid frontiers of good and evil. Good and evil exist in the same continuum. Whatever is good, by the very nature of its goodness, harbors a grain of evil. This is a guarantee against any exaggerated sense of moral superiority which goodness by itself may entail. The notion of perfection, therefore, is alien to African thought. Perfection in itself constitutes a temptation to danger, an invitation to arrogance and self-glorification. The principle of balance defines the relationship between good and evil. As life operates in a dialectics of struggle, so also does good balance evil and *vice versa*.

1

General Introduction

Ivor Agyeman-Duah

Christopher Columbus is well revered in Western history dealing with "discoveries." There are of course gross inexactitudes of what he claimed to have found as he navigated his ways and by-ways in the Americas, the new world and Asia from the 1470s. Between the kings of Portugal, Don Juan, and the king and queen of Spain (symbols of the two maritime powers of the time), who competed and struggled for influence, power and territories in the Christian world and beyond, Columbus was the envoy of suspicion, the Admiral of the Ocean Sea and Viceroy over all 'the lands he discovered.' Whatever the conclusion of Columbus' life ambition, he ended up as a defining personality in historical geography. The minuses aside, he had at least one country in Latin America, Colombia (not to mention the many cities and towns across North America), named after him. I need explain at this point that the definition for Latin America here is the cultural region of the American continent made up of countries where the official and predominant language is Latin-based—Spanish, Portuguese, or French. From a comfortable social and political perspective, it is the independent countries consisting of Mexico, which is located in North America, virtually all the countries of Central America, a lot of the countries in South America and the islands of the Caribbean which have Spanish, Portuguese, French or admixtures of these in the popular Creole varieties. Following this line of definition, Latin America is comprised of 20 independent countries with Brazil as the biggest.

In Santo Domingo, in the Dominican Republic for the 23rd Annual Meeting of the Association of Third World Studies (ATWS), I joined as part of the recreation some participants in a tour guide's view of the capital. In the Old City, as they call the historical part of Santo Domingo, the guide, with a limited mastery of the English language, pointed his hand at a hill indicating where Christopher Columbus lived with his wives, passed away and was buried. He was very sure of that. Not White and definitely a man of color—most likely with black ancestry. I later asked this guide what Columbus means to him. Obviously, he was not enthused. Blackness is an invocation of the stereotypes in Santo Domingo. You do not see it in the streets or as a form of outward racism since, of course, there is a large population of Black people. It lies in the mentality or consciousness of especially the middle and ruling classes. That accounts for why Haitians are disliked, despised, and called names here.

One of the conference participants, William E. Berry, an African-American who teaches at the University of Illinois in the United States, spent some time in Santo Domingo doing research and considers himself Black, as he does in the United States. He soon realized that he was not really considered Black but nearer to a classification of Spanish or White because of his light complexion. One day, as he did his regular walk in the sun, a concerned citizen asked him why he would do that to darken his skin complexion. It was then that he realized that he hardly saw people with light complexion walking in the afternoon as a choice or a form of recreation. It is better to preserve their light complexion than to make it Black.

The Mass Media and the Globalization of Racial Prejudice: Representations of Africa and Blackness in Newspapers in the Dominican Republic (2005) was a presentation that William Berry gave to illuminate the negativity and 'backwardness' of Blacks in the country as captured in the media—the same abhorrence Africans find in the negative reportage of Africa by Anglo-Saxons in Europe and the United States. If that was a shock to William Berry when he started his research work, it was a shock to some of us as well.

The presence of Africans or Blacks in the Western Hemisphere preceded Columbus. Why then is it that Black people never seem to be assimilated into many of the societies in the sense of full acceptance culturally and politically? In a 2005 population estimate of Caribbean countries and colonized lands, the colonized territory with an estimated population and percentage of Africans turned out this way, according to Paul Goodwin, Jr. (2005):Anguilla 13,254 (100%); Antigua and Barbuda 68,722 (91.3%); Aruba, 71,566 (83.7%); Bahamas 301,790 (85.0%); Barbados 279,254 (85.0%); Belize 279,457 (24.9%); Bermuda 65, 365 (58.0%); Cayman Islands 44,270 (20.0%); Cuba 11,346,670 (11.0%), Dominica 69,029 (89.2%); Dominican Republic 8,950,034 (11%); Grenada 89,502 (82.0%); Guadeloupe 448,713 (90.0%); Haiti 8,121,622 (95.0%); Martinique 432,900 (90.0%); Montserrat 432,900 (90%), Netherlands Antilles 219,958 (85.0%); Puerto Rico 3,916,632 (8.0%); Saint Kitts and Nevis 38,958 (95.0%); Saint Lucia 166,312 (90%); Saint Vincent and the Grenadines 117,534 (77.4%); Trinidad and Tobago 1,088,644 (39.5%); and Turks and

Caicos Islands 20,556 (90.0%). Obviously, this source undercounts the total African populations in the Caribbean in light of Bangura's more complete data in his first of two chapters in this book.

These islands, by no means exhaustive and with population from as small as almost 10,000 people to as big as almost 11 million, have in many cases more than an average African presence. Although slavery and colonialism from the 1600s (in some cases before) accounted for population growth rate, long before these events, which go before even Columbus 'discovery,' Blacks or Africans had been around. There is of course evidence of this in the most vital way that people express themselves—culture!

In Michael Coe's *Mexico*, there is a photograph of large carved heads. Plates 12 and 13 are particularly illustrative of the presence of Africans and the influence they had in the country. It dates from 1200 to 900 BC and says the following: "The early formative sculptures of San Lorenzo include seven colossal Heads of great distinction. These are up to 9 feet 4 inches in height.... it is believed that they are portraits of mighty Olmec rulers, with heavy, thick-lipped, rather 'Negroid' features" (Coe, 1977: 71-73).

In Basil Davidson's *The Lost Cities of Africa*, one reads that "Omari, in the 10th chapter of his *Masalik al-absad*, reproduces a story which suggests that Atlantic voyages were made by mariners of West Africa in the times of the Emperor Mansa Musa of Mali (who got to power in 1307 and went on to the Hajji in 1324 ...' Omari records the answer of the Sultan to questions posed by Ibn Amir Hajib as folows:

> .... The monarch who preceded me would not believe that it was impossible to discover the limits of the neighboring sea. He wished to know. He persisted in his plan. He caused the equipping of 2000 ships and filled them with men, and another such number that were filled with gold, water and food for two years.... They went away, and their absence was long ... Then a single ship returned.... The captain: "Sultan, we sailed for a long while until we met with what seemed to be a river with a strong current flowing in the open sea. My ship was last. The others sailed on, but as each of them came to that place they did not come back nor did they reappear; and I know not what became of them. As for me, I turned where I was and did not enter that current (Davidson, 1970:74-75).

When people talk about globalization today, it is as if it is a new phenomenon. But Columbus on his third voyage realized or at least so the evidence points that there were already trade relations between Africa and Latin America. Ivan Van

Sertima writes in his *They Came Before Columbus: The African Presence in Ancient America* that

> On his third voyage he came upon more evidence of the contact between Guinea and the New World. From a settlement along the South American coast on which his men landed on Tuesday, August 7, the natives brought 'handkerchiefs of cotton very symmetrically woven and worked in colors like those brought from Guinea, from the rivers of Sierra Leone and of no difference. These handkerchiefs, he said, resembled almayzars-Guinea headdresses and loincloths. Each one is a cloth so woven in colors that it appeared an almayzar with one tied on the head and the other covering the rest (Sertima, 1976: 18).

Before this, the assurance had been given of the existence of the islands in South America by among others Africans who had through trade and adventure visited there before Columbus. Sertima observes:

> The building of the new city of Isabella, the struggle to subdue and convert the natives of the Caribbean (who had massacred the first settlement of Spaniards and demolished their fort), occupied most of Columbus's time until his return from his second voyage in 1496. While in Española, however, something happened that confirmed and complemented what Don Juan had said. The Indians gave proof that they were trading with black people. They brought to the Spanish concrete evidence of this trade. The Indians of this Española said there had come to Espanola a black people who have the tops of their spear made of metal which they call gua-nin, of which he [Columbus] had sent samples to the sovereigns to have them assayed, when it was found that of the 32 parts, 18 were gold, 6 of silver and 8 of copper (Sertima, 1976:13).

Almost two decades after Van Sertima's work, more excavations led to the discovery of new stone heads, including a very old one that has a seven-braided Ethiopian hairstyle. According to an issue of the *Journal of African Civilization*, far more complex analyses of the contacts between African and American towards the close of the Bronze Age (circa 948-680B.C), could now be presented of ancient African astronomy, map-making, scripts, navigation, trade route, pyramidal structures, linguistic connections, technological and ritual complex (*Journal of African Civilization*, 2006).

Marika Sherwood, a distinguished researcher of the Institute of Commonwealth Studies in London, even goes back to African presence in Europe and how their contribution influenced many European activities in Europe and the Americas. In her unpublished essay, "The Multi-ethnic History" (2006), she writes:

> As evidenced by the innumerable vase-paintings, paintings, jewelery, etc, the Greek 'civilization' consisted of multi-ethnic peoples. People from around the Mediterranean lived in Greece, as did Africans (as they did in Italy) and participated in society at all levels, from gods to generals to slaves. (Slaves, incidentally, came from all ethnic groups.).... Some historians, both modern and ancient (including, for example, Herodotus), have argued that Africans have colonized Greece before the rise of what we call 'Greek civilization'. Greek scholars certainly visited Egypt, and some claim, Greek philosophy has its roots in that of Egypt (Sherwood, 2006:1).

There is also in Sherwood's essay Africa's contribution to Roman rule and civilization. The Romans garrisoned their empire using troops from subject territories such as among the Gauls, Belgians, Asturians and Thracians. As Sherwood puts it, "The Romans eventually conquered all of the North Africa littoral, used their African subjects and captives in their western outpost. There is archaeological and other evidence (including written sources, for example the *Historia Augusta*, and many inscriptions) of Africans in the Roman armies in Britain. Such evidence has been found in London, York, Moresby, and South Shields ..." (Sherwood, 2006:2). Indeed, this high level of globalization, even if the term was not used at the time, showed that Africa's civilization through trade, pure adventure, military campaign, politics—whether Africans were colonizers of some European societies or the colonized—was not restricted to Africa.

It is also the case that Africa as the spot of humanity from where other races sprang might certainly have found some of its kin crossing by natural necessities to Latin America and beyond before and after the sea trade. After all, Ayi Kwei Armah tells us in his memoirs, *The Eloquence of the Scribes* that

> In outline, the African goes as follows: human life, according to available evidence, began on the African continent, most likely in the east and central plateau regions. From there the first human communities spread outward to populate the world. In time some settled in the Nile valley. At first they created small, autonomous and ineffective communities, vulnerable to the elements. The geographical configuration of the Nile valley, featuring a powerful river, the longest, flowing through the largest of deserts, with periodic floods and droughts, was such that communities living in original scattered, uncoordinated pattern of settlement had little chance of survival, and none at all of prosperity (Armah, 2006:15).

Armah's assertion only endorses what the famous Egyptologist, Anta Diop, says:

> The suddenness and volume of the flooding of the Nile obliged the first African populations, whom chance had brought to this valley, either to rise above individual, clannish and tribal egoisms or to disappear. Thus emerged a supra-tribal authority ... with the power necessary to conduct and coordinate irrigation and water distribution works essential to the general activity. Thus was born a whole hierarchic body of functionaries ..." (Anta Diop, 1991:130).

This emphasis on the spread of humanity was very gradual. Even though it affected Latin America, it is difficult to assess, as it is with all areas of migration at that period, to get an exact number of the Blacks or Africans in the region. It certainly might have been small compared to the number of slaves in the region.

These help constitute some of the earliest traces of evidence of Africans in the Caribbean or the Americas. Twenty years after the period of discovery in the 1470s, the Spanish and the Portuguese had known of African artifacts. In the oral traditions of Native Americans, African folklore and traditions registered. These are undisputable. Eric Williams, in *From Columbus to Castro-the History of the Caribbean*, authoritatively asserts: "There is sufficient evidence available today of immigration of the Vikings via Greenland in the North, while it is thought that Africans had direct contact with South America before Columbus sailed for 'the Indies' in 1492" (Williams, 1970: 18).

The second phase of the African presence in Latin America represented the fruits of all that the Portuguese and Spanish kings and their professional or freelance sailors sought to gain. It had to do with economic glory and, thus, of wealth that sprang from the conquest of others. Economic consideration disguised as religion and a civilizing mission of so-called backward people fueled the political and scientific desires to visit and dominate other regions. Columbus was definitely not just interested in taking risk with the voyages. There were silver and gold in South America, as trade between Africans and the natives had shown. Columbus had also signed an agreement with the Spanish Sovereigns before he left, specifically agreeing on his share of silver and gold. He wrote in his journal on November 12 1493: "Without doubt there is in this land a vast quantity of gold ..."

Once these expectations had been ascertained, a massive transportation of human cargo to help the plantation economy of the 'masters,' silver and gold digging for the Spanish and Portuguese in South America took place. This was the basis for prosperity of these two countries to be later joined by the British and French. Of course the labor was largely from Africa. At the time, the slave trade with the Portuguese was more than a half century old (before the 16th Century). The Spanish were also engaged in the purchase of Africans. As Williams says,

> For this reason, and also because of the constant anxiety to keep the colonies immune from heresy, the Spanish Government turned to the Negro slaves in Spain, who had been converted to Catholicism. The king initiated the Negro slave trade on September 3 1501 … Unlike the mortality of the Indians, however, Negro mortality meant merely obtaining more Negroes from Africa.… The introduction steadily increased. In 1517 the first asiento, or contract, was arranged for the importation of four thousand Negroes in eight years into the West Indies. In 1523 the king ordered the provision of another four thousand into all the Spanish dominions, of which fifteen hundred were to go to Hispaniola, five hundred to Puerto Rico and three hundred each to Cuba and Jamaica. In 1528 Cuba requested a further seven hundred. In the same year a contract was signed with two Germans for the importation of four thousand slaves into the Caribbean colonies in four years.… thirty thousand was later imported into Hispaniola alone by 1540, and more then a thousand into all the Spanish dominions (Williams, 1970: 41-42).

I do not intend in this brief expose to do a detail recollection of how many of these geographical spaces were populated with enslaved Africans and the influence they had on Latin America. The small African population in the 1400s that traded with the people in Latin America and exchanged cultural pleasures had by the late 1500s transcended into a huge labor force. Spanish historian Herrera, in his *History of the Indies*, could afford to write the following: "There are so many Negroes in this island, as a result of the sugar factories, that the land seems an effigy or an image of Ethiopia itself" (Herrera, 1977:18).

The transportation of enslaved Africans to the Eastern Caribbean, Jamaica in particular, has a telling effect on the linguistic development in that country. Many scholars, including Abdul Karim Bangura in this book, have produced great scholarship to show the origins and current state of African language varieties in the Caribbean and the African language varieties spoken in many of the countries in Latin America and the Caribbean. Ashanti/Asante folklore, like the Ananse stories, the history of Yoruba divinities and other globalized folklore in Henry Louis Gates, Jr.'s *The Signifying Monkey: A Theory of African-American Literary Criticism,* in which he develops the notion of 'signifying,' a linguistic tradition using Black culture in describing things or people by the use of humor, paradox, indirection, boast and insult, are a part of the history of the African presence in Latin America (Gates, 1983). The dimensions are clear with respect to geography: Africanisms in the literatures of Francophone, Hispanohone,

Anglophone and Creole trace their roots to Africa. Apart from the area of culture, we cannot underestimate the influence this history had on the politics of the people who emerged as leaders within Latin America and beyond it like Eric Williams, George Padmore, Frantz Fanon, Walter Rodney and Fidel Castro.

In the early 1990s, the 500th anniversary of Christopher Columbus' "discovery" of the Americas was celebrated across the academic terrains in the world. The "discovery" was followed by five centuries and two decades with slavery, colonialism and neo-colonialism with Spain and Spanish culture still supreme in many ways. Africa or Black culture has managed to live alongside the cosmopolitan might of Spanish dominance. But Spanish colonialism was destructive in uprooting factors of production—land and capital, especially not to talk of labour, which, of course, was cheap. The traditional land tenure system in the Americas was tampered with as a reflection of the motive of the king of Spain 600 years ago. Wealth in the form of land and capital has since circulated among the descendants of the Spanish conquerors and generated rootless growth. Descendants of Africa and other people of color have for hundreds of years been at the receiving end.

In Todaro's popular book, *Economic Development in the Third World*, a better picture is painted: approximately 1.3% of landowners in Latin America hold 71.6% of the entire area of land under cultivation. If Mexico, Bolivia and Cuba, countries that have carried out drastic land reforms since the early 1900s are excluded, Latin America agrarian structure seems to follow a uniform pattern. This is basically one in which a small number of Latifundious control a large proportion of the agricultural land while a vast number of the Minifundios must scratch a survival existence on a meager fraction of the occupied land (Todaro, 1997:302).

Three hours after the guided tour of Santo Domingo, we went to the city center where we found the brisk informal economy at play. Dominated by Blacks that have Krobo features from Ghana and Ibo facial expression of Southeastern Nigeria, they sold dog chains, maps of the country and T-shirts (not that every Black person is poor). In a typical African inspired shop that I visited, there were made in Africa sculpture pieces. Some imported from Africa while others were a blend of the creativity and influence of Africa's minds. The shopkeepers, Black like me, kept smiling as they did to the other Africans from Cameroon and Nigeria. We admired and could easily identify with the art works. They told us that the pieces were real African art. When we referred to the fact that they were made in the Dominican Republic and that they were not from Africa, one of the keepers told us: "Yes, made in Dominican Republic but by artists who have African ancestry, haven't been to Africa but create with the spirit of Africa." If nothing remains, at least there is the creativity of African art and linguistic influence in Latin America.

2

Caribbean Historiography

Mario D. Fenyo

The most complete historiography of the Caribbean, to-date, is found in Vol. VI of the *General History of the Caribbean*, subtitled "Methodology and Historiography of the Caribbean," published by UNESCO and edited by B. W. Higman (1999). In addition to a series of historiographical essays, it includes a bibliography of 216 pages. The only publication comparable to this undertaking is the critical bibliography produced single-handedly by Gordon K. Lewis titled *Main Currents in Caribbean Thought: The Historical Evolution of Caribbean Society in its Ideological Aspects, 1492-1900* (1983).

The scarcity of comprehensive bibliographies should not surprise us. The very notion of the Caribbean as a "region" is fluid. Depending on the discipline, on the nationality of the author, on certain subjective factors, the Caribbean may be said to have a core area, sometimes referred to as the "islands," as the Antilles (Greater and Lesser) or as the West Indies. The latter term may or may not correspond to the former British colonies. Peripheral regions are sometimes attached to this core, especially in recent literature. These may include the islands of the Bahamas and Turcos and Caicos, both of which lie in the Atlantic Ocean, the eastern shores of Central America, extending from Belize in the north, sometimes even from the Yucatan peninsula, to the southern boundary of Panama, and the northern coast of South America, to include not only the coastal areas of Colombia and Venezuela, but also Guyana, French Guyane and Suriname—the last three not bathed by the waters of the Caribbean. For the sake of feasibility and convenience, my convenience, this chapter is a brief discussion of the "core" as defined above. Even so, the task of the historian or of the historiographer is daunting, since the region includes anglophone, francophone, and hispanophone islands, as well islands where Dutch, Creole, Papiamiento, and other local languages are spoken, and even written; nowadays "creolization" is promoted on several islands, in addition to the half island of Haiti.

Of course, the region has a so-called "prehistory" beginning with the first settlement by Native American groups, including the Arawak and the Carib; this has been largely the domain of archaeologists. It is also possible to view the history of West Africa and of the Atlantic World Market as part of the "prehistory" of the Caribbean, since the overwhelming majority of the population in the islands, including those that emphasize their Spanish heritage, can trace their ancestry to the African continent. The African roots and the transference of African cultures have been studied since the seminal works of Roger Bastide, translated into English in 1971 as *African Civilizations in the New World* and of Melville J. Herskovits, particularly his *Myth of the Negro Past* (1941).

"Diaspora studies" have taken over some of the space in the study of Africana; while they seldom limit themselves to the Caribbean, the archipelago occupies large segments in these studies, for obvious reasons (see, for instance, Vincent Bakpetu Thompson's *The Making of the African Diaspora in the Americas 1441-1900* (1988). There is, moreover, an East Indian Diaspora, which has been largely overlooked.

From the middle of the 20th Century, the islands have become island-nations or island-states; each has acquired a historical identity different from all the others. Since nationhood entails the evocation or even the construction of a past, the political balkanization of the region has resulted in the balkanization of its history.

Moreover, the history of the Caribbean is also part of the history of certain distant regions. At one time, it has been argued, the wars in the Caribbean were a reflection or microcosm of European wars involving England, France and Spain. Since the Spanish-American war and the so-called "corollary to the Monroe Doctrine" enunciated by Theodore Roosevelt, the region is often regarded as the *mare nostrum* of the United States, which has acquired direct control over Puerto Rico and the Virgin Islands, and has intervened directly and militarily around the region. It could even be argued that the Caribbean played a major role in the Cold War, between 1945 and 1990, with Cuba challenging the hegemony of the United States.

Nevertheless, a number of authors have attempted to produce a more or less coherent history of the region. The first and most subjective of these is by the Spanish clergyman and "defender of the Indians," Bartolome de Las Casas; the first volume of his *Historia de las Indias* dates from 1520 (reprinted in three volumes in Mexico by Fondo de Cultura in 1951). It gave rise to considerable polemics, especially on the part of Spanish historians who describe Las Casas as the inventor of a fiction, *la leyenda negra*. The work of Las Casas was followed by that of Gonzalo Fernandez de Oviedo, *Historia general y natural de las Indias* (1st ed. 1535, reprinted in Madrid by Ediciones Atlas in 1959). The French counterpart of these early works on the Caribbean is Charles de Rochefort's *Histoire naturelle et morale des Antilles de l'Amérique* ... (1658).

Although a geographer, Carl Ortwin Sauer has produced a well researched history of the Caribbean in the 15ᵗʰ and 16ᵗʰ Centuries entitled *The Early Spanish Main* (1966). Eric Williams, the founding father of Trinidad and Tobago and the author of the widely disseminated and oft translated *Capitalism and Slavery* (1964) and of other historical works—all of them pertinent to the Caribbean—was among the first to attempt a general history, entitled *From Columbus to Castro: the History of the Caribbean* (1970). More progressive in its tone and politics is the work of Juan Bosch, one-time president of the Dominican Republic, with roughly the same title: *De Cristobal Colón a Fidel Castro: el Caribe frontera imperial,* dating from the same year (1970). For a more recent edition (1981), see the one published by Casa de Las Americas in Habana, Cuba.

Franklin W. Knight, who has succeeded in compressing the history of the region into a rather thin volume entitled *The Caribbean: The Genesis of a Fragmented Nationalism* (1978), has also edited Volume 3 of the UNESCO production, under the title *The Slave Societies of the Caribbean* (1997). More voluminous than Knight's brief treatment, Gordon K. Lewis's *Growth of the Modern West Indies* (1968) is by now a classic.

Special mention must be made of J.H. Parry and P. M. Sherlock's *A Short History of the West Indies* (1956); it was among the first to overcome the Eurocentric presentation of the region as a backwater of European wars and imperialism, in favor of a more Caribbean point of view. Since the publication of their work, the term "discovery" as applied to the Americas, or to the Caribbean in particular, has become problematic.

It is not possible to discuss the historiography of individual islands or countries here; I must content myself with mentioning a few seminal works—proceeding from the Northwest to the Southeast. For instance, the work of Cuban law professor, economist and ethnologist Fernando Ortiz, especially his *Hampa afrocubana: Los negros esclavos* (1906), is remembered for opening up the study of the culture of the African diaspora on an international scale.

For Haiti, there exists a plethora of distinguished works focusing on or around the Haitian revolution, but the masterpiece produced by the Trinidadian C.L.R. James, *The Black Jacobins; Toussaint L'Ouverture and the San Domingo Revolution* (1938), remains standard. Many outstanding historians have written on Jamaica, but Orlando Patterson deserves special mention as a thinker and politician; as regards Jamaica, his main work is entitled *The Sociology of Slavery: an Analysis of the Origins, Development, and Structure of Negro Slave Society in Jamaica* (1967). There are also many deserving works on the history of Puerto Rico, but Arturo Morales Carrión has earned special mention, not only because he was above the political fray, but also because he reaches out to other nations, particularly in his *Puerto Rico and the non-Hispanic Caribbean* (1952).

Among the monographs on the smaller islands, George Brizan's book on Grenada titled *Grenada, Island of Conflict; from Amerindians to People's Revolution, 1498-1979* (1984) stands out. The fame of R. H. Schomburgk rests not only on the library named after him, but also on his *The History of Barbados* (1971, 1st ed. 1848). Of course, his research has been superseded by many others, including the wide-ranging works of Edward Kamau Brathwaite. On Trinidad and Tobago, Eric Williams deserves credit once again for writing the first comprehensive work, *History of the People of Trinidad and Tobago* (1962). Those who followed his lead include Bridget Brereton, who has written on almost every aspect of the culture and history of Trinidad and Tobago. The best known historian to come out of Guyana is Walter Rodney, who has earned martyrdom as a consequence of his assassination, especially since historians usually shy away from confrontation and danger. He demonstrated the thoroughness of his research in *A History of the Guyanese Working People, 1881-1905* (1981).

For detailed discussions of individual historians of the Caribbean, their works, their islands, the *General History of the Caribbean*(1999), referred to earlier, will be invaluable. Since the publication of this six-volume history, there has been a rather steady stream of works dealing with the Caribbean, often with an economic or economic history bent. Apart from the flow of works on post-revolutionary Cuba, the preferred format nowadays seems to be the collection of essays, resulting from some international conference. *Caribbean Survival and the Global Challenge* (2002), edited by Ramesh Ramsaran, is one example. Another is *Banana Wars: Power, Production and History in the Americas* (2003), edited by Steve Stiffler and Mark Moberg, which takes advantage of another trend—i.e. monographs focusing on a single, albeit important, crop or commodity.

3

African Linguistic Connections

Abdul Karim Bangura

Introduction

The paucity of works on this chapter's topic is exemplified by one of the most popular texts used in courses dealing with African linguistics entitled *African Languages: An Introduction* (2000) edited by Bernd Heine and Derek Nurse. As the editors confess in the introductory chapter of the book, they were unable to treat African-Diasporic linguistic connections in the way they merit. They also state that when some of their colleagues asked them to devote some space to aspects of African linguistic influences in the Americas, they settled for asking John McWhorter to write a brief overview for them. The following is all McWhorter writes on the topic:

> The principal fate of African languages in the New World has been to serve as primary sources for the creoles which slaves developed in plantation colonies. Often speaking closely related languages while having minimal contact with whites, early slaves' transfer-laden approximations of a given European language conventionalized into new languages, African-derived as much as European. The most extreme manifestations are Surinam creoles, whose syntaxes are broad reproductions of Kwa ones: the Saramaccan *di nákináki dágu bi wáka gó a wósu báka* 'the beaten dog walked behind the house' superimposes English lexicon on Kwa features such as a reduplicated attributive adjective, verb serialisation, and a postposed nominal as spatial deictic. Other creoles include Gullah, Haitian, Papiamentu and the extinct Negerhollands.
>
> Lighter African influence can be seen in the speech of many Afro-Hispanics, whose speech diverges slightly from local Spanish varieties in features such as a double negator pattern (*no lo tengo no* 'I don't have it') found in Kongo. Popular Brazilian Portuguese is similar, in idiom calques such as *o dia ta limpo* 'The day is clean' for 'It's dawn,' an expression found also in Yoruba. These New World Iberian varieties, as well as creole in general, also preserve many West African lexical borrowings.

Evidence suggests that African slaves did not usually transmit their native languages to following generations. A notable exception is in Brazil, where Fon, Kongo, and Yoruba were maintained by communities of blacks, the latter into the twentieth century. More typically, African languages were preserved in fossilised ritual registers often kept today, such as Twi and Gbe in Jamaica; these two and Kongo in Surinam, and Mende in the Sea Islands of South Carolina (Heine and Nurse, 2000:9-10).

That this effort, while commendable, is inadequate for comprehending the extent of the African linguistic connections in the Diaspora is hardly a matter of dispute. And as Max Black observes, "Language ... appears as the very stuff of which 'ideas' are made. To separate thought from its symbolic manifestations would be as futile as to try separating a mind from its embodiment in a human organism" (1969:17). Thus, since an overwhelming majority of Caribbean countries' populations are African and mixed African and other ethnic Caribbeans, ranging from 18.9 percent in Puerto Rico to 100 percent in Anguila (see Table 1), there is a great deal more to be said about African linguistic connections in the Caribbean.

Table 1: Population Estimates, 2005

Country or Colonized Territory	Estimated Total Country Population	Percent of Population African	Percent of Population Mixed African and Other(s)
Anguilla	13,254	100.0%	—
Antigua and Barbuda	68,722	91.3%	2.4%
Aruba	71,566	83.7%	—
Bahamas	301,790	85.0%	—
Barbados	279,254	90.0%	6.0%
Belize	279,457	24.9%	—
Bermuda	65,365	58.0%	—
Cayman Islands	44,270	20.0%	40.0%
Cuba	11,346,670	11.0%	51.0%
Dominica	69,029	89.2%	—
Dominican Republic	8,950,034	11.0%	73.0%

Table 1: Population Estimates, 2005 (Continued)

Country or Colonized Territory	Estimated Total Country Population	Percent of Population African	Percent of Population Mixed African and Other(s)
Grenada	89,502	82.0%	13.0%
Guadeloupe	448,713	90.0%	——
Guyana	438,144	10.0%	31.0%
Haiti	8,121,622	95.0%	4.0%
Jamaica	2,731,832	90.9%	7.3%
Martinique	432,900	90.0%	——
Montserrat	9,349	90.0%	——
Netherlands Antilles	219,958	85.0%	——
Puerto Rico	3,916,632	8.0%	10.9%
Saint Kitts and Nevis	38,958	95.0%	——
Saint Lucia	166,312	90.0%	6.0%
Saint Vincent and the Grenadines	117,534	77.4%	19.0%
Surinam	756,283	36.0%	7.0%
Trinidad and Tobago	1,088,644	39.5%	18.4%
Turks and Cacois Islands	20,556	90.0%	——
Virgin Islands, British	22,643	83.0%	——
Virgin Islands, United States	108,708	78.0%	9.9%

Sources:
Indexmundi.com Online
CIA World Factbook Online
Antigua.barbuda.com Online
Goodwin, Jr. Paul, ed. 2005. *Global Studies Latin America* 12th ed. Guilford, CT: McGraw-Hill/Dushkin
Epodunk.com Online
Population Reference Bureau prb.org Online

Accordingly, the purpose of this chapter is to discuss the linguistic connections between African languages and African Language Varieties (ALVs) in the Caribbean. The name ALVs is a cover term employed in this chapter to refer to a continuum of varieties whose features (depending on which end of the continuum one considers) may be very similar to or very different from those languages in Africa. The name ALVs is used in acknowledgment of the fact that these varieties are spoken primarily by and among African and mixed African and other ethnic Caribbeans. Nonetheless, it is imperative to note that not all African and mixed African and other ethnic Caribbeans are speakers of ALVs and not only them speak the languages. Indeed, a language a person speaks is not in any way predestined but is instead determined by the language to which s/he is exposed. So, just as a person born in Port-au-Prince does not automatically become a speaker of French, an African Haitian is not predestined to become a speaker of Kweyol. Similarly, a member of a different ethnic group who is exposed to Kweyol as his/her first language will likely become a speaker of Kweyol.

While these varieties are defined in terms of ethnicity, other demographic variables such as age, areas of residence, gender, socio-economic status, and style influence ALVs in the Caribbean, as they do other language varieties. An 80-year-old Aruban speaker of Papiamento/u will speak differently from a 14-year-old Papiamento/u speaker. A male Surinamese speaker of Saramaccan will likely have different features in his speech than a female Saramaccan speaker. A Yoruba speaker in Cuba will speak differently from a Yoruba speaker in Trinidad and Tobago. And it is likely that a middle-class Belizian speaker of Garifuna will have different features compared to a working-class Garifuna speaker. Moreover, no individual speaker of an ALV speaks the same way all the time. Instead, one varies his/her speech depending on style and context.

In order to paint a substantive picture of the connections between African languages and ALVs in the Caribbean, many linguistic aspects are explored in the rest of this chapter. These include the origins and current state of the ALVs in the Caribbean, cultural basis for African linguistic tendencies in the Caribbean, African language usage, salient linguistic features, African idiomatic expressions, African linguistic impact on Caribbean literature, and *ausbau* and *abstand* considerations. In the end, conclusion is drawn based on the findings.

Origins and Current State of African Language Varieties in the Caribbean

The origins of ALVs in the Caribbean have been an issue of great debate among linguists. The debate hinges upon two theories: the Dialectologist and the Creolist. Out of these two theories has also emerged a unified perspective. These views are described in the following three subsections.

The Dialectologist Theory

The Dialectologist school of thought posits that ALVs trace their roots back to the varieties of European languages. Beginning around the 1920s and continuing into the 1940s, dialectologists presented the first scholarly analyses of ALVs, arguing that these languages should be analyzed in terms of regional differences, just like other varieties of European languages (see Figure 1). Essentially, it was believed that African Carribeans spoke the languages of Europeans with whom they shared comparable socio-economic and regional backgrounds.

```
African                           African Language Varieties
Languages  →  Pidgin  →  Creole  →  in the Caribbean

                    Pidgin
Earlier             Modern Standard European Languages
European    →       Nonstandard Varieties of European Languages
languages           (including African Language Varieties in the Caribbean)
```

Figure 1: The Dialectologist Hypothesis

The Creolist Theory

The Creolists challenge the Dialectologists by arguing that ALVs trace their roots back to the times of the slave trade when Africans from regions such as Angola, Ghana, The Gambia, Guinea, Ivory Coast, Mali, Nigeria, Senegal, and Sierra Leone were forced together on slave ships with no common language among them. They were exposed to many different African languages, such as Bulu, Hausa, Wolof, and Twi, as well as the European languages of the ships' sailors (see Figure 2). In most instances, enslaved Africans were isolated from speakers of their own native languages in order to avoid possible uprisings. Consequently, enslaved Africans were forced to develop some common form of communication.

Out of this language contact emerged a Pidgin language—i.e. a speech system that is formed to provide a means of communication between people who do not share a common language. As the enslaved Africans formed communities on the slave plantations of the southeast Atlantic seaboard, this Pidgin became the primary means of communication for many of the enslaved. When a Pidgin becomes the principal language of a speech community, it is referred to as a Creole. According to Creolists, increased contact between speakers of this Creole and speakers of other European language varieties resulted in the decreolization (change in a Creole that makes it more like the standard language of a territory) of this language, which has led to the present-day ALVs.

African Languages → Pidgin → Creole → **African Language Varieties** in the Caribbean

Earlier European Languages → Pidgin
Modern Standard European Languages
Nonstandard Varieties of European Languages

Figure 2: The Creolist Hypothesis

To support their theory, Creolists analyze features found in ALVs that resemble European language-based Creoles of the Caribeban such as Jamaican Creole or Creoles of Africa such as Krio spoken in Sierra Leone.

The Unified Perspective

For many years, linguists were radically divided between the Dialectologist and Creolist theories concerning the roots of ALVs. The issue remains unresolved to this day. However, it appears that movement is being made toward an understanding of ALVs that accepts some reasoning from both schools of thought (see Figure 3). Put differently, proponents of the unified view believe that the Dialectologist and Creolist positions may not be mutually exclusive, but instead both may contribute to the understanding of the origins, history, and development of ALVs in the Caribbean.

African Languages → Pidgin → Creole → Modern Standard European Languages
African Language Varieties in the Caribbean

Earlier European Languages → Pidgin
African Language Varieties in the Caribbean
Modern Standard European Languages
Nonstandard Varieties of European Languages → Other **African Language Varieties** in the Caribbean

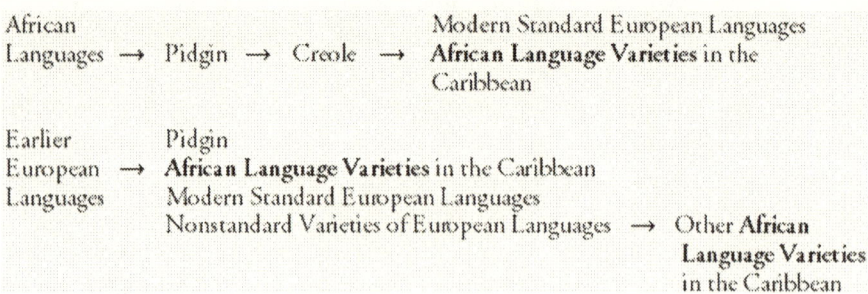

Figure 3: The Unified Approach

A profitable question then is the following: What are these ALVs and how did they emerge in the Caribbean? To answer this question, a country-by-country profile is provided as depicted in Table 2.

Table 2: African Language Varieties Spoken by Country

Country or Colonized Territory	African Language Varieties
Anguilla	African-English Creole
Antigua and Barbuda	African-English Creole
Aruba	Papiamento/u
Bahamas	African-English Creole Haitian African-French Creole/Kweyol
Barbados	African-English Creole/Patois
Belize	Garifuna African-English Creole/Kriol
Bermuda	African-English Creole/Slanguage
Cayman Islands	African-English Creole/Patois
Cuba	Yoruba Haitian African-French Creole/Kweyol Arará Congo/Bantu Abakwa/Ñañigos Jamaican African-English Creole/Patois
Dominica	African-English Creole African-French Creole/Kweyol
Dominican Republic	African-Spanish Creole Haitian African-French Creole/Kweyol
Grenada	African-French Creole/Patois
Guadeloupe	African-French Creole/Kweyol
Guyana	African-English Creole/Creolese
Haiti	African-French Creole/Kweyol

Table 2: African Language Varieties Spoken by Country (Continued)

Country or Colonized Territory	African Language Varieties
Jamaica	African-English Creole/Patois Twi Yoruba Kikongo Mahi (Also varieties of these languages referred to as Nago, Tambo, and Goombeh)
Martinique	African-French Creole/Kweyol
Montserrat	African-English Creole
Netherlands Antilles	Papiamento/u Haitian African-French Creole/Kweyol Dominican Republic African-Spanish Creole
Puerto Rico	African-Spanish Creole/Bozal Creole
Saint Kitts and Nevis	African-English Creole
Saint Lucia	African-English Creole African-French Creole/Kweyol
Saint Vincent and the Grenadines	African-French Creole/Patois

Surinam	African-English Creoles:
	  Sranan Tongo
	  Ndyuka
	  Aluku
	  Paramaccan
	  Kwinti
	  Guyanese African-English Creole/Creolese
	African-Portuguese Creoles:
	  Saramaccan
	  Matawai

Trinidad and Tobago	African-English Creole African-French Creole/Kweyol Yoruba Kikongo Hausa Fon

Table 2: African Language Varieties Spoken by Country (Continued)

Country or Colonized Territory	African Language Varieties
Turks and Caicos Islands	African-English Creole Dominican African-English Creole Dominican African-French Creole/Kweyol Haitian African-French Creole/Kweyol
Virgin Islands, British	African-English Creole/Calypso
Virgin Islands, United States	African-Danish Creole African-Dutch Creole African-English Creole

Sources:
Too many to be listed here; they are cited throughout the chapter.

In Anguilla, or Snake Island, African-English Creole, the creation of enslaved Africans and the British, is spoken. The island was first colonized by English settlers in 1650 and incorporated into a single British dependency along with the neighboring islands of Saint Kitts and Nevis in the early 19th Century (www.nationmaster.com). Enslaved Africans were first introduced to Anguilla immediately after the colonization.

African-English Creole, created by enslaved Africans and the British, is spoken in Antigua and Barbuda. Sir Christopher Codrington and others brought enslaved Africans from Africa's west coast in 1685 to work the plantations. The enslaved Africans were emancipated in 1834 but remained economically dependent on the plantation owners (www.state.gov, www.tiscali.co.uk).

Papiamento/u is spoken in Aruba. The language combines words and patterns from West African and Native American languages, Portuguese, Dutch, Spanish, French and English. Portuguese slave traders first brought Papiamento/u to Aruba and the islands of the Netherlands Antilles from the west coast of Africa. The name Papiamento/u itself means "jibber jabber" in its own language. However, today, the language is spoken by Arubans of all social classes. Even though Dutch is the official language of Aruba, many children do not learn it until they go to school where they also learn English, Spanish, and German (www.mandurotravel.com).

In the Bahamas, African-English Creole and Haitian African-French Creole/Kweyol are spoken. In the 18th Century, British loyalists (enslaved Africans, English Puritans and other immigrants) who left New England due to increasing anti-British sentiments moved to the Bahamas, bringing with them the African-English Creole that is closely related to the Gullah African-English variety of South Carolina. Haitian immigrants also speak the Creole/Kweyol on the islands (www.nationmaster.com, www.bahamas.com).

African-English Creole/Patois is spoken in Barbados. The language was developed due to the forced mass migration of enslaved Africans to the island in the late 1600s and 1700s. While the Queen's English is the "official language," African-English Creole/Patois remains the most commonly used (www.rough-guides.iexplore.com).

Garifuna and African-English Creole/Kriol are spoken in Belize. The Garifuna language is the creation of the Garifuna, also known as Caribs or Black Caribs. It is a mixture of African and Native Carib languages of the Lesser Antilles. In the early 1800s, the Garifuna, who descended from shipwrecked Africans that escaped from enslavement, arrived in Belize. The Garifuna had resisted British and French colonialism in the Lesser Antilles until they were defeated by the British in 1796. After putting down the violent Garifuna rebellion on Saint Vincent, the British moved between 1,700 and 5,000 of the Garifuna across the Caribbean to the Bay Islands (present-day Islas de la Bahia) off the north coast of Honduras. From there, they migrated to the Caribbean coasts of Nicaragua, Honduras, Guatemala, and the southern part of present-day Belize. By 1802, about 150 Garifuna had settled in the Stann Creek area, present-day Dangriga, and were engaged in farming and fishing. Other Garifuna later came to the British settlement of Belize after finding themselves on the wrong side of a civil war in Honduras in 1932 (fotw.vexillum.com, bleasesswebworld.com, www.belizeans.com).

Belizean Creoles have created their own language they call Kriol, which they consider to be a completely distinct language that evolved from but no longer an English dialect. The Creole of Belize are the offspring of enslaved Africans imported to work the logging camps and European adventurers. Most of the enslaved Africans came from West Africa, between the present countries of Angola and Senegal, via Jamaica. Many of the Europeans came from Scotland and North Britain. While a majority of the Creole population claims an enslaved African/European ancestry, Asians, East Indians, Garinagu and Mestizos have all intermarried with Creoles and have adopted the Creole culture (www.southern-belize.com).

African-English Creole/Slanguage is spoken in Bermuda. The language was the creation of enslaved Africans first brought to the islands in 1616 and the British. It is spoken and understood by all Bermudans (www.bermuda-online,org).

African-English Creole/Patois is spoken in the Cayman Islands. It is the creation of enslaved Africans and British who had intermarried. From 1670 to 1962, the Cayman Islands were effective dependencies of Jamaica. By 1999, 38-40 percent of the population of the Cayman Islands was of Jamaican origin (www.nationmaster.com).

In Cuba, Yoruba, Haitian African-French Creole/Kweyol, Arará, Congo/Bantu, Abakwa/Ñañigos, and Jamaican African-English Creole/Patois are spoken. These languages derive from the enslaved Africans whom the Spaniards imported well into the 16th Century and later migrations. The Africans were brought from across the west coast of Africa, although they were boarded at major ports. From there, beginning on shipboard, the several nationalities would have to learn one another's languages, and their cultural expressions would mix over time in some ways, or retain their characteristics in other ways. The largest group among these Africans was the Yoruba, frequently subsumed under Lucumi, from what is now Nigeria. The Arará from what is today Benin (Dahomey) were numerically smaller than the other groups, but they were respected for the power of their gods. They are known especially in Palanzas province. From present-day Angola and the Republics of the Congo came the second largest group called Congo or Bantu, whose beliefs, with the associated ceremonies, came to be known as the Regla Mayombe, or Regla de Palo (Palo Monte). Also from what is today Nigeria, from the sacred lands around the river Calabar, came the Abacuá (Abakwa), or Ñañigos.

In the 1790s, Haitian African-French Creole/Kweyol made itself known in Oriente, the eastern end of the island and the closest to Haiti. French colonialists on the island of Hispaniola fled Haiti as a result of the Revolution, in which the former enslaved Africans took power. The nearness of Cuba to Haiti and the similarities between the sugar plantation economies of the two countries made Cuba a natural place for the evacuating French to go. They arrived with the enslaved Africans they managed to keep, who in turn brought their language with them (www.lafi.org). More recently, Cuba is perhaps the only country that has welcomed so many Haitians fleeing the persecution of the Generals and their savage regime. There are an estimated 300,000 recent Haitian arrivals in Cuba. And Haitian African-French Creole/Kweyol, which is till spoken by Haitiian descendants of the earlier waves, is Cuba's second major language (www.afrocubaweb.com). Also, in more modern times, many Jamaicans arrived in Cuba, not as enslaved Africans but as salaried workers for the cane fields (www.lafi.org).

African-English Creole and African-French Creole/Kweyol are spoken in Dominica. The African-English Creole was the creation of Africans, from areas inland beyond the coast region that extended from what is today Senegal down to Angola, who were brought across the Atlantic ocean to work on the sugar and coffee plantations of Dominica from the early 1700s up till 1807 and the British. Two other periods of African arrival refreshed the linguistic influences from across the Atlantic. After the first stage of Emancipation in 1834, a small group of workers from West Africa voluntarily agreed to contract themselves out to come and work in Dominica for wages and settled near some estates. Then in 1837 and at other times around those years, ships carrying enslaved West Africans across the Atlantic Ocean and destined for colonies and states where slavery had not yet been abolished were captured by the British Royal Navy. The enslaved Africans were disembarked on the islands including Dominica and were liberated. Some African family names that were handed down from generation to generation are still present in Dominica: e.g., Akie, Cuffy for Kofi, Carbon for Gabon, Quamie, Quashie, and Africa (www.lennoxhonychurch.com).

Dominica's African-French Creole/Kweyol was the creation of enslaved Africans and the French. While the island was a British colony, it also had a population that was strongly influenced by France. The French absorbed, exchanged and influenced the ways of the enslaved West Africans more than the British. The attitude of the two colonizers was difference: On the one hand, the French controlled by absorbing and mixing the foreign culture with their own; on the other hand, the British, through laws and subtle social rules, attempted to control by wiping out everything and replacing it completely with their own culture. The French families in the scattered estates triumphed over the British colonialists huddled in Roseau, as did Catholicism over the Church of England (www.lenoxhonychurch.com). Kweyol speakers are predominantly rural folk. Since the 1950s, parents in the urban centers, anxious for their children to speak only English—seen as a means of social mobility, have discouraged its use. However, every year, Dominicans and Saint Lucians celebrate Kweyol or the traditional Creole language and culture. For one week in October, they dress in Kweyol fashion, and on one day they speak only in Kweyol. The sounds of Kweyol permeates the entire Dominican society and has become part of the consciousness of even those who are not primarily Kweyol speakers, as the language and culture are intertwined (www2.unesco.org).

In the Dominican Republic, African-Spanish Creole and Haitian African-French Creole/Kweyol are spoken. The African-Spanish Creole was the creation of enslaved Africans brought during the first half of the 16th Century to work the island's gold and silver mines, which were swiftly exhausted, and the Spaniards. The country has had a history of changing ownership, with Spain, France, Haiti,

Spain again, and the United States (twice) taking their turns at ruling Dominican territory amid attempts at independence and self-rule. Haitian African-French Creole/Kweyol can be heard in many parts of the Dominican Republic because of the many Haitian migrants and their descendants. In recent years, illegal immigration from Haiti has worsened as Haiti's population explodes and the Dominican economy improves (www.tiscali.co.uk, language.school-explorer.com).

African-French Creole/Patois is spoken in Greneda. Interestingly, while English is the official language in Grenada, the African-French Creole/Patois is also very common among the residents. The latter language was the creation of enslaved Africans and French colonialists. Early attempts by both British and French to subdue the Carib on Grenada failed, and it was not until 1650 that the French established a foothold on the island. The French carried out a campaign of extermination against the Caribs. When defeat was inevitable, the last small group of Carib jumped to their deaths from a northern cliff instead of being enslaved. Enslaved Africans were then brought in to work the sugar plantations. The British ousted the French from Grenada in 1762 but were driven out in 1779. France held the island for four years until the Treaty of Versailles (1783) awarded it to Britain. In 1795, an uprising by enslaved Africans provoked bloody reprisals. When slavery ended in 1883, contract workers from Africa and India began to arrive in Grenada (granada.caribbeanway.com, www.kuoni.co.uk).

In Guadeloupe, African-French Creole/Kweyol is spoken. The language is the creation of enslaved Africans who were brought to Guadeloupe in the 1600s and French colonialists. It is the result from the oral tradition and conveyed by story-tellers who, during the evening meetings, used to listen to the young and the old's tales and stories of tradition. It is more than a language. It is also a way of life and the history of people, evoking at the same time Africa, enslavement, but also dance, music, islands, feasts, etc. (www.lonelyplanet.com, www.webcaraibes.com).

African-English Creole/Creolese is spoken in Guyana. The first enslaved Africans, drawn from different ethnic groups in the 1600s, developed a rudimentary pidgin to communicate with one another. On arrival in Guyana, they added some words and expressions drawn from the language of their Dutch masters; and as time passed, this African-Dutch Creole went through a metamorphosis. As a new generation of enslaved Africans was born in the country, African-Dutch Creole became the first language of these children who continued to add new words and expressions to it. As such, the development of what is referred to as "Creolese" intensified. When eventually the English took control of Guyana, the enslaved Africans added more and more English words and expressions to their vocabulary; and with succeeding generations, the African-Dutch Creole eventually disappeared. However, some Dutch words remained in the now African-English Creolese, as did some from the French language (www.guyana.org).

In Haiti, African-French Creole/Kweyol is spoken. The language was the creation of enslaved Africans and the French. By 1512, the Spanish had all but wiped out the Tiano (Arawak) who inhabited what was then called Hispaniola (Little Spain). Unable to withstand enforced labor and European diseases, the Tiano died in appalling numbers. The use of European indentured servants proved fruitless, setting up the cycle of the importation of enslaved Africans from West and Central Africa that began in 1517. In 1697, the French acquired the western third of the island of Hispaniola. Over the next century, a plantation economy developed and enslaved African labor made Saint Domingue (Haiti) the wealthiest colony in the entire world (www.neworleansmistic.com).

Haiti's African-French Creole/Kweyol has emerged as the true national language of the Republic of Haiti. In addition to seven million people in the country, it is also spoken by about a million Haitians living abroad. All Haitians speak the language, although a small minority of about 10 percent of the population also speaks French, which they have learned either at home or at school. Nonetheless, even Haitians who are fluent in French consider Haitian African-French Creole/Kweyol, which they employ for most everyday communication, as the symbol of their national identity (www.indiana.edu).

In Jamaica, African-English Creole/Patois, Twi, Yoruba, Kikongo, Mahi and a varieties of these languages referred to as Nago, Tambo and Goombeh are spoken. The Jamaican African-English Creole/Patois was the creation of enslaved Africans and the British. For the other ALVs, as Maureen Warner Lewis observed in 1979, "Apart from Twi elements which have persisted over four centuries, the other languages have a separation in time from their mainland matrices of no more than a century and a half. For this reason, the languages other than Twi persist not only as lexical items, but are articulated by their speakers with varying levels of syntactic competence and sophistication" (1979:101).

The Arawak people were living on the island of Jamaica when the Spanish arrived. By about 1650, the Arawak had almost completely disappeared. They died from new diseases brought by the Spaniards and from hard, forced labor required by their conquerors. The Spanish soon realized that they needed more workers for the plantations, so they brought enslaved Africans to work in the colony. Suddenly, in 1655, a British expedition arrived on the island and seized it from the Spaniards, who released the enslaved Africans and left the island. Many of the freed Africans disappeared into the mountains. Known as Maroons, many remained free and cultivated their own way of life. The British brought more enslaved Africans to work the sugarcane plantations. In 1938, all slaves were declared free. Many African Jamaicans chose not to work on the plantations, so the British plantation owners brought indentured workers from Central Africa, India, China, and Britain (www.sbgmusic.com).

African-French Creole/Kweyol is spoken in Martinique (www.nationmaster.com). The language is the creation of enslaved Africans and the French. When the French began to colonize Martinique in 1635, they also started to import enslaved Africans to the island to work on the plantations.

African-English Creole is spoken in Montserrat. The language is the creation of enslaved Africans, enslaved Irish and the British. Montserrat was populated by the Arawak and the Carib when it was claimed by Christopher Columbus for Spain in 1493, naming the island after the mountain of the same name near Barcelona, Spain. In 1632, the island fell into the control of the British. The importation of enslaved Irish and West Africans followed during the 1600s and 1700s. Montserrat was briefly captured by France between 1782 until 1783, when it was returned to Britain under the Treaty of Versailles (en.wikipedia.org).

In the Netherlands Antilles, made up of the islands of Bonaire, Curaçao and Sint Maarten, Papiamento/u, Haitian African-French Creole/Kweyol and Dominican Republic African-Spanish Creole are spoken. As stated earlier in the discussion of Aruba, Papiamento/u was derived from various African, Dutch, English, French Portuguese, Spanish and Native American languages. It is to this day the predominant language in the Netherlands Antilles, especially in Bonaire and Curaçao; since 1989, it has been taught in primary schools. Like Aruba, Bonaire and Curaçao were originally populated by the Arawak and the Carib when the Spanish arrived in the 16th Century. Unlike Aruba, however, which was largely left alone by the Spanish, Bonaire and Curaçao were settled from 1527. The Arawak and the Carib were wiped out and replaced as plantation labor by imported enslaved Africans (uk.encarta.msn.com, www.factmonster.com).

In Sint Maarten, whose culture has its roots largely in African, Dutch and French influences, one can also hear Haitian African-French Creole/Kweyol and Dominican Republic African-Spanish Creole being spoken. This is the result of the arrival of recent immigrants from Haiti and the Dominican Republic seeking employment in the booming tourist industry. In fact, only about 20 percent of the residents in Sint Maarten is comprised of people born on the island (webcenter.travelaol.com).

African-Spanish Creole/Bozal Creole, the creation of enslaved Africans, Native Americans and Spaniards, is spoken in Puerto Rico. The Tainos ruled the island when the Spanish arrived and took it over in 1493. During their 400-year rule, the Spanish replaced the Tainos with enslaved Africans to work in the fields (www.gotopuertorico.com). Many of these enslaved Africans were from the Congo, and the rest were from Ashanti and 31 other groups in Central and West Africa. It is believed that many of them were brought through the island's east side, resulting in the large populations of African Puerto Ricans in San Juan and Vieques. Ponce and Mayaguez also have large African Puerto Rican populations that came from Columbia, Cuba and Haiti. During the years of slavery, miscegenation was rampant. Tainos were raped by Spaniards and intermarried with the incoming enslaved Africans (www.absoluteastronomy.com).

In Saint Kitts and Nevis, African-English Creole, the creation of enslaved Africans imported into the islands in the 1600s and 1700s and the British, is spoken. Saint Kitts became the first British colony in the West Indies in 1623. Anglo-French rivalry grew in the 17th Century and lasted more than a century. In 1783, by the Treaty of Versailles, the islands of Saint Kitts and Nevis were definitively awarded to Britain (www.britanica.com, www.state.gov).

African-English Creole and African-French Creole/Kweyol are spoken in Saint Lucia. The first language is the outgrowth of the languages of the enslaved Africans and English, and the second language is an amalgamation of the languages of the enslaved Africans and French. Although the African languages were suppressed as soon as the enslaved Africans arrived on the island, French planters still needed to communicate with their workers and, gradually, the common language of Saint Lucian Creole, Kweyol, also called patois, evolved, heavily laced with African as well as English and French grammar and vocabulary. Despite the fact that it has only recently appeared in written form, there is already a Saint Lucian Creole translation of the Bible (www.nbportal.com). Saint Lucia's first known inhabitants were the Arawak. Europeans first landed on the island between 1492 and 1502 during Spain's early exploration of the Caribbean. The Dutch, English and French all tried to establish trading outposts on Saint Lucia in the 17th Century but were challenged by the Carib. The English, with their headquarters in Barbados, and the French, centered on Martinique, found Saint Lucia attractive after the sugar industry developed in 1765. Britain eventually triumphed, forcing France to permanently give up Saint Lucia in 1815 (www.state.gov).

African-French Creole/Patois, the outgrowth of the languages of the enslaved Africans and the French, is spoken in Saint Vincent and the Grenadines. The

Carib, who were the original inhabitants of the island, aggressively prevented European settlement on Saint Vincent until the 18th Century. Enslaved Africans, whether shipwrecked or escaped from Saint Lucia and Grenada and seeking refuge in Saint Vincent, intermarried with the Carib and became known as Black Carib. Beginning in 1719, French colonialists cultivated coffee, cotton, indigo, sugar and tobacco worked by enslaved Africans. In 1783, Saint Vincent was ceded to the British under the Treaty of Versailles. Conflict between the British and the Black Carib continued until 1796, when General Abercromby crushed a revolt fomented by the French radical Victor Hughes. More than 5,000 Black Carib were subsequently deported to Roatan, an island off the coast of Honduras (www.state.gov).

In Surinam, six Africa-English Creoles (Sranan Tongo, Ndyuka, Aluku, Paramaccan, Kwinti, and Guyanese African-English Creole/Creolese) and two African-Portuguese Creoles (Saramaccan and Matawai) are spoken. Sranan Tongo, Surinam's lingua franca, and the other six Maroon languages, were derived from the languages of the enslaved Africans who fled between 1712 and 1800 and English. Saramaccan and Matawai were derived from the languages of the enslaved Africans who fled between 1690 and 1710 and Portuguese. The template for the African contributions included languages spoken in Togo, Benin, eastern Ghana, the Congos, and northern Angola. In an eight-year period, the enslaved African population had increased ten-fold: in 1683, there were an estimated 1,000 enslaved Africans in Surinam; by 1691, almost 10,000 more had been transported to the island. Between 1651 and 1830, an estimated 215,000 Africans were again transported to Surinam. Guyanese African-English Creole/Creolese is spoken by a substantial number of people in the western rice growing district of Nickerie in Surinam (Forte, 2003:1-8).

During the so-called "Indian Wars" (1678-1684), when the Arawak sensed an opportunity to get rid of the colonizers, they started attacking them fiercely. The colony was thrown into complete chaos, giving the impetus to marronage in that period. Marronage or the establishment of villages in the forest by escaped Africans began in the 17th Century. The Maroon monopolized the trade between the interior Arawak and the coastal Europeans. The Maroons then developed Ndyuka to facilitate trading between themselves and the Trio, the Wayana and the Carib (Forte, 2003:3).

African-English Creole, African-French Creole/Kweyol, Yoruba, Kikongo, Hausa and Fon are spoken in Trinidad and Tobago. The first two languages, the Creoles, were the creation of enslaved and immigrant indentured African laborers, and the British and French, respectively. The major spoken language in Trinidad and Tobago is the African-English Creole. The African-French Creole, which was once the most widely spoken language on the island, is now rarely heard (en.wikipedia.org; Warner Lewis, 1979:101).

Before European contact, the island of Trinidad was inhabited by the Arawak and the Carib, and Tobago was occupied by the Carib. In the early 1500s, the Spanish settled on Trinidad while Tobago frequently changed hands between the European sea powers: British, Courlanders, Dutch, and French. During the Napoleonic wars, Britain consolidated its hold on both islands and combined them into the colony of Trinidad and Tobago in 1889. Enslaved and free indentured African laborers were imported to supply labor in the 19th and early 20th Centuries (en.wikipedia.org).

In the Turks and Caicos Islands, African-English Creole, Domican African-English and African-French Creoles, and Haitian African-French Creole/Kweyol are spoken. The Turks and Caicos African-English Creole was the creation of enslaved Africans and the British. The first inhabitants of the islands were the Taino who were eventually replaced by the Lucayan, who by the middle of the 16th Century were virtually wiped out by European diseases brought by the Spaniards and also through enslavement. The 17th Century saw the arrival of settlers who established themselves on Grand Turk, Salt Cay and South Caicos. Enslaved Africans were brought in to rake the salt for the British colonies in America, and were later joined by the British Loyalists fleeing the American Revolution. In 1776, after being controlled by the British, French and Spaniards, Turks and Caicos became part of the Bahamas colony; but attempts to integrate them failed and were abandoned in 1848 (en.wikipedia.org).

Dominican African-English and African-French Creoles and Haitian African-French Creole can also be heard on the Turks and Caicos Islands because they are now the home of expatriates from Dominica and Haiti. The total population of Turks and Caicos Islands is approximately 25,000, of which Grand Turk has about 6,000 and Providenciales 15,000. The rest is made up of the expatriate population, among whom Dominicans and Haitians have a substantial representation (www.savory-co.com, www.welcometothecaribbean.com).

African-English Creole/Calypso, the creation of enslaved Africans and the British, is spoken in the British Virgin Islands. The islands were initially occupied by the Arawak and the Carib. By 1555, they were invaded by Europeans; and by 1596, most of the indigenous population had been decimated by European diseases and forced labor. Dutch buccaneers held Tortola until it was captured by English planters in 1666. The English established a plantation economy on the island, and for the next 150 years developed the sugar industry through the labor of enslaved Africans. As soon as slavery was abolished in 1838, leading to the rapid faltering of the plantation economy, the majority of the white population left for Europe (www.montrosetravel.com).

In the United States Virgin Islands, African-Danish Creole, African-Dutch Creole and African-English Creole are spoken. These languages were the creation of enslaved Africans and Danish, Dutch, British and Americans, respectively. For nearly 3,000 years, the Tiano and the Carib inhabited the United States Virgin Islands. After Christopher Columbus claimed the islands for Spain in 1493, the inability of the Spaniards to defend them in the 1500s and the 1600s led other European powers to begin settling there. In the 1600s, the French were joined by the Dutch and the English. In 1671, Denmark clearly ruled Saint Thomas; in 1685, it signed a treaty that allowed the Brandenburg American Company to start a slave-trading post on the island. At about the same time, Saint Thomas became a refuge for pirates. But piracy ceased to be a factor in the island's economy in the early 19th Century, and the slave trade continued until 1848. Most of the enslaved Africans were captured along the Gold Coast (present-day Ghana) from the Amina, Ashante, Igbo, Mandika and Wolof ethnic groups. By 1695, Saint Croix was under the control of the French, but the colonists had moved on to what is today Haiti. As trade increased between 1700 and 1750, prosperous merchants replaced the pirates on Dromigens Gade (Main Street) in Charlotte Amalie. By 1718, the Danish settlements had expanded to Saint John and a fort was constructed in Coral Bay. In 1733, Denmark purchased Saint Croix from France, uniting the three Virgin Islands. The United States purchased the islands in 1917 and placed them under the administration of the United States Navy; the United States Department of Interior later took over the administration of the islands (www.virginisles.com, stjohnlinks.com, www.fodors.com).

Modern speakers of the African languages say listening to the ALVs in the Caribbean is like hearing Old English, for example. These African languages froze in time with the enslaved Africans' arrival in the Caribbean. In countries where enslaved Africans were smaller in number, as in Puerto Rico, it was harder to retain their languages. In countries where the number of enslaved Africans was larger, as in Cuba, they were able to form African cultural and religious societies which still exist today (www.cubanet.org).

Cultural Basis for African Linguistic Tendencies in the Caribbean

As Franklin Knight and Margaret Crahan inform us, during the long period of the social disintegration, reconstruction and nation building that ensued throughout the Caribbean in the 19th and 20th Centuries, Africa's legacies became distorted, diluted and subordinated to those of Europe. Communication between Africa and the Caribbean virtually disappeared. Even worse was that Africa's legacies became relegated to an inferior status even among the predominantly African Caribbean societies. A conflict emerged between the Eurocentric goals and attitudes of the proponents of "high culture" and the mass-based, African Caribbean "low culture." The conflict, which is especially evident in language and literature, continues to plague the Caribbean societies to this day. While colonialism might have succeeded in driving underground the strong appeal of Africa throughout the Caribbean, it nevertheless was unable to destroy the bonds between the two regions. As ideal, refuge and solace, an image of Africa remained alive and well among its descendants in the New World. The image remained very important because the African origin could not be completely expunged from those fundamental areas of society and culture that form the basis of every community and that are expressed in its language, literature and religion (1979:16).

And as Harry Hoetink recounts, enslaved Africans, awaiting their transportation overseas and thrown together in the slave-trading ports, came from many African anthrocultures, with their own languages and religions. A similar situation held on the plantations. To ensure their survival, the enslaved Africans had to master languages in which they could understand themselves and their overseers. The trauma of forced uprooting probably stimulated this psychological impulse. The acquisition of a new medium of social communication must have occurred with great speed. For instance, in a few decades after 1667, enslaved Africans of Dutch masters had developed the English-influenced Sranan in Surinam. With every adaptation to a new territorial system, language as a medium of indispensable social communication must have changed in chameleon fashion. The Creole languages that evolved in the Caribbean only in rare cases (Aruba, Curaçao, Bonaire) acquired the status of a general "vernacular," encompassing the entire population. They became part of a boundary marking territorial anthroculture—a development which must have been forced by the fact that the dominant strata in these small islands consisted of linguistically varied groups which, in their mutual contact, employed Papiamento/u as a *lingua franca* of their own, thereby liberating it from social stigma. In the British and French colonies, as well as in Surinam, the Creole languages remained associated with the lower strata, despite the fact that the metropolitan languages were subject to creolization. In the Portugues and Spanish colonies, the creolized metropolitan languages became generally adopted, with social and regional variations well within one linguistic span (1979:27).

Hoetink then provides and defines the following three concepts as being useful for general analytical purposes (including the analysis of material culture) and *a fortiori* for the study of the social configurations with which African Caribbean culture is linked, and which in shorthand fashion may be alluded to as that of the African, the enslaved, and the Black:

> (a) *anthroculture*, commonly identifying a territorial social system; (b) *socioculture*, as a product of class; and (c) *ethnic group*, as a social category, sometimes coinciding with class, which within a social system has a recognizable identity of its own based on anthrocultural attributes (sometimes including descent) (1979:26-7).

For Hoetink, language change, adoption, and invention not only showed a remarkable flexibility, as far as language was employed as a medium of communication inclusive of those who were not enslaved, but also a similar linguistic inventiveness was used precisely to exclude outsiders. As a functional or class stratum, enslaved Africans sometimes developed secret codes that the masters and overseers could not understand. Special language laden with African vocabulary was also employed when communicating with the supernatural. Where enslaved Africans or later immigrants from one African language were able to preserve their language in mutual contact (e.g., Cuba, Brazil, Jamaica, and Trinidad and Tobago), speakers of African languages born in the Western Hemisphere still exist (1979:28).

The very wide diffusion and similarity of ego- and body-oriented elements that exist everywhere in African America, their apparent strong resistance to local adaptation and their relative inflexibility, argues Hoetink, must be understood both in terms of the very early reflexive type of learning with which these elements are associated and in terms of a type of behavior and belief that are common to the different anthrocultures of West Africa. The concept of a Western African grammar, he adds, comes to play here, and might be adopted, if full emphasis is accorded to the notion of generational transmission. Thus, according to Hoetink, "If one were to denote the culture common to the Afro-American population as a whole, in terms of unadulterated 'Africanisms,' these ego- and body-oriented elements should be considered its most important attributes. (This is not to say that all these attributes are still the exclusive property of Afro-Americans; several of them have been adopted, in the course of a creolization process, by other groups in varying breadth and intensity.)" (1979:30).

Hoetink adds that

Between the vehicular function of language and religion, and the ego-orientation of the type of behavior [common to the different anthroculture of West Africa], music, song, and dance occupy an intermediate position. Here a common "grammar" or motoric and rhythmic elements, mutually recognizable and adoptable within the Afro-American societies, combines with an impressive variety in melodic structure in form and instrumentation, strongly influenced by non-African tradition and creole innovations, although different in each individual society. It is perhaps this intermediate position with its curious and unique "blending" which has resulted in a gradual adoption by all strata and in all Afro-American societies of some music, song, and dance forms. This distinctive variety per society made them at the same time an important attribute of each creole anthroculture (1979:30-31).

Furthermore, according to Hoetink, from the first day of contact on, there already existed a "we" consciousness among the African group, largely coinciding with that of the enslaved stratum. The "we" feeling was maintained and reinforced over and above the development of functional differentiations within the group of enslaved origin. It seems as if in the course of the processes of functional differentiation and cultural creolization, terms such as *bakra, buckra, macamba*, etc. as early references to the white master evolved in the Caribbean societies. These concepts first referred to white persons in general, and then to the exogenous, or recently arrived, white. In other societies, such as Martinique, the term *beke* kept its original meaning. In Curaçao, a common territorial norm in characterizing the outsider only became accepted in the 20th Century: *jiu di Korsow* (child of Curaçao). But in a more recent phase of this society's increasing polarization, the internal division is denoted by further differentiating between *bon jiu di Korsow* (good children of Curaçao: the African and the mixed Africans with others) versus *jiu di Korsow* (all others) (1979:36).

Indeed, a remarkable development was that Africans in the Caribbean fought to maintain their cultural tradition by forming clubs called *Nations* in all the islands. Each nation had a mandate to preserve African languages, cultures, music and religions. The ALVs are alive and well today because of the persistence of their speakers. Today, these languages enjoy prominence; and in some societies such as the Netherlands Antilles, there are government sponsored attempts to document the language and to create dictionaries. The use of the pen by African writers (Griots), the use of African poetry, calypso and reggae music, etc. are all elements of the contemporary resistance movement that mirror that of the enslavement period. Although some aspects or early resistance culture have crossed over to pop culture, these vehicles often reflect a duality. They are in fact still used to defy much of the colonial (and neo-colonial) baggage Caribbean Africans still carry (husky1.stmary.ca).

African Language Usage

In her survey of Yoruba usage in Trinidad during the 19th Century, Maureen Warner Lewis delineates five ways the language was employed. These five ways, which are discussed in the following paragraphs, further indicate the impact of African languages on the culture and psychology of the Caribbean peoples. What emerges is a picture that suggests ambivalent attitudes of resentment and accommodation that include the pragmatic concession of an immigrant people to objective social reality; at the same time, it is a picture that illustrates faith in mystical redemption from an alien law and social environment (1979:102-3).

First, Yoruba was used for group communication. But since the immigrants spoke various dialects of the language, dialect-switching aided communication and increased as each new generation was born into a more complex dialectal community. While this dialectally heterogeneous Yoruba remained the in-group language, the African-French Creole, the colony's *lingua franca*, began to usurp this domestic role. This development placed pressure on the African minority to conform to Creole social norms, especially because the African community was itself fragmented along linguistic and cultural lines. Living a peasant existence in scattered semi-isolated linguistic communities, or in cosmopolitan ghettos, 19th Century Africans in Trinidad had little need for English, the official language, except in rare instances such as when they encountered the law (Lewis, 1979:103).

Second, Yoruba was employed as a secret code because it was not understood by the society at large, thereby becoming a powerful tool of in-group identification. "They abused the police in it, they warned each other against police raids, they pleaded their cause before God for redemption from 'the sons of the whites who brought us here.' 'Every dog must have his day,' the warned" (Lewis, 1979:103-4):

> K'a maa wo
> K'a maa w'oria
> B'oyinbo l'oke
> Olopa b'otun
> Sesa maa wo
> Abelube won se

Caught between *oyinbo* (the whites—rulers) and *olopa* (police—agents of the rulers), they called upon their *orisa* (deities, saints) to help them survive (Lewis, 1979:104).

Third, Yoruba was used to complain about slave labor and of paltry wages. Parents complained about their children being alienated from them, born as they were under the white man's flag, and growing up amid strange languages and customs. For these Africans, their children being born into slavery was the most disturbing development in their lives. All of these emotions of bitterness were expressed in their own tongue (Lewis, 1979:104).

Fourth, Yoruba was the medium for the speakers' deepest prayers and desires. It was, and continues to be, explicitly stated that Yoruba is more "powerful" than any European language. Even on Christmas day, grandparents blessed their grandchildren in Yoruba. The language was used for morning and evening prayers, for safety and success. Yoruba songs were needed to properly dispatch the dead. Yoruba chants and salutations with ancient esoteric references accompanied animal sacrifices during religious ceremonies. Hundreds of chants praising the *orisa* retained, and to this day are still employed by Trinidadians to worship them (Lewis, 1979:104).

Finally, according to Lewis, Yoruba was used to contribute dirges and secular songs. Some of these songs carry historical references to the wars and social upheavals in Yorubaland in the 19th Century (1979:104).

An addendum to Lewis' five ways an African language was used in the Caribbean is as a tool for business transactions. In Guyana, for instance, Africans brought with them the art of bargaining. It is a linguistic art to be mastered, as it is considered an insult to lose in a bargain (Craighton, www.guyanaundersiege.com).

Salient Linguistic Features

Salient linguistic features of ALVs that have been observed can be classified into the following categories:

Phonological Features

(1) Consonant cluster simplification or reduction: e.g., in Jamaican African-English Creole, girl > gyal

(2) [r] > [y] in word/syllable-medial positon: e.g., in African-French Creoles, Creole > Kweyol

(3) *um um*, a verbal pause while the person thinks what to say in Bermudan African-English Creole for example

(4) Use of high (′) and low () tones to distinguish between certain pairs of words: e.g., in Papiamento/u, *sálà* (living room), *sàlá* (to salt); *blàhá* (to travel), *bláhà* (voyage)

(5) [θ] > [t] in word/syllable position: e.g., in Jamaican African-English Creole, thing > ting

(6) y-insertion and t-deletion: In Jamaican African-English Creole, [ant] > [yan], as in can't > kyan

(7) w-insertion: e.g., in Jamaican African-English Creole, boy > bwoy

Morphological Features

(1) Past tense markers: In English, the past tense is mostly formed by adding a suffix, [t], [d], or [ed], given the final sound of the verb base. If the base ends in a consonant, the addition of the past tense suffix may create a consonant cluster. Instead of using a suffix like [ed], the African-English Creole speaker in the Caribbean would put the word *deh* before the verb. The same is done in African-French Creole/Kweyol by adding *te* before the verb to indicate past tense.

English	African-English Creole
I walked	*me deh walk*
She talked	*she deh talk*

(2) Plural markers: In English, plural is mostly marked by adding a suffix, [s], [es], [en], given the final sound of the word. Instead of using a suffix like [s], the Papiamento/u speaker would use the same morpheme from the third-person pronoun, *nan* (they), at the end of the word.

English	Papiamento/u
children	*muchanan*
men	*machunan*
women	*muhenan*

(3) Reduplication is used with different functions: e.g., in Papiamento/u, *pega-pega* (stick-stick) is a reptile that sticks to people; *poko-poko* (slow-slow) means careful, very slow, annoyingly slow; *tan-tan* (time-time) means in the meantime; *pushi-pushi* (cat-cat) refers to quietly, as when a teenager is sneaking off to meet a date at 2:00 A.M.

(4) *la*-emphasis: In African-French Creole, *la* (there) is added after the noun for emphasis: e.g., *key-la* (that there house)

Syntactic Features

(1) Gender indication: In Papiamento/u, most nouns have no special form to indicate gender. Gender is created by adding the words *homber* (man)/*machu* (male) or *muha* (woman) behind the noun. The following are examples:

pushi machu	cat male (male cat)
mucha homber	child male (male child or boy)

(2) Non-plural nouns: In Papiamento/u, nouns do not denote plurality when prefaced with a word with plural meaning. Examples:

un homber	one man
dos homber	two men
un hende	one person
hopi hende	many people
un strea	one star
tres strea	three stars

(3) Verb number distinction: In Papiamento/u, verbs have no distinction of number. Examples:

Ami ta bai	I am going
Nos ta bai	we are going

(4) Time and aspectal verbs: In Papiamento/u, to indicate time and aspect, verbs use particles which stand on their own. Examples:

Mi ta bai	I am going
Mi tabata bai	I was going
Mi lo bai	I will go

(5) Serial verbs: In Papiamento/u, there is a presence of serial verbs. Examples:

sinta pensa (un ratu)	sit and think (for a while)
lanta para wak	stand up stand look

(6) Active versus passive voice: In Papiamento/u, there is a preference for the active voice rather than the passive. Examples:

Nan ta ferf e kas	They are painting the house
Nan ta straf e muchanan	They are punishing the children

Lexical Features

Certain African words have become a staple in ALVs in the Caribbean and also in European languages.

Word	Meaning
okay/O.K.	from Mande *o ke*, meaning that's it or all right, and Wolof *waw kay*,
banjo/banja	which means all correct
yam	from Kimbundu, meaning a stringed musical instrument
duppy	from Twi *anyiam* and Fulani *nyami* ("to eat"), edible, starchy, tuberous
zombie	root
mocko jumbie	from from Kongo, which means ghost
akra	from Kongo-ngola *nzumbi*, meaning deity or fetish
da-da/da	from Kongo meaning healer
doucouna/cankie	from Yoruba *akara*, an oily cake made from grounded beans and fried
okra	from Ewe, meaning an elder care-taking sister
obeah	from Akan *dokona*, which means sweet mouth or sweet thing
sensay costume	from Igbo *okworo*, a young green pod about four to six inches long,
su-su/sou-sou	noticeably ridged and pointed with slimy seeds and flesh used as a
tosh	boiled vegetable
Oluboku	from from Twi *o-bayo-fo*, from Nembe *obi*, from Igbo *obi*, and from Ibibo
tumba	*abia*, meaning a set of secret beliefs in the use of supernatural forces to
wawa	attain or defend against evil ends
zarabanda	from Twi *sense*h, a type of fowl with curled or ruffled feathers
bata	from Yoruba, which means a fund in which many people pool their
itotele	money

Word	Meaning
okonkolo/omole	from Kikongo, Ci-Luba and other Bantu languages in West Africa, asso-
nganga	ciated with the verb -tuta, -tota, meaning to carry, pick up, or load
gombey	from Yoruba which means drum of peace
afe-la	from Kongo meaning drum
	from Twi, a large tree climbing yam with a widely spreading root system
	from Kongo meaning the god of iron
	from Yoruba denoting drum
	from Yoruba, a type of talking/rhythm drom
	from Yoruba, a type of talking/rhythm drum
	from Kongo, meaning bowl or basket
	from Kongo, meaning rhythm and drum
	from Ewe afe a, meaning the house

African Idiomatic Expressions

By confining her comparison to Yoruba and Trinidadian African-English Creole, Maureen Warner Lewis traces the provenance of idioms and concepts in the latter language, without denying the parallel occurrence of such idioms in other West African languages as well. The following are two examples from her text (1979:105-6):

Yoruba:	Enia ni.
Literal translation:	Human being he is.
Trinidadian African-English Creole:	He is people (too).
Gloss:	An assertion of humanity. The individual is worthy of regard.

Yoruba:	Ohunkohun.
Literal translation:	Thing + connective + thing.
Trinidadian African-English Creole:	T'ing and t'ing.
Gloss:	... and so on and so forth.

Lewis discovers that linguistic correspondence can be traced even further. She also finds that pace, idiom, phrase length, and sequence of mood in the following quarrel in Yoruba she extracted from a popular printed serial in Western Nigeria in 1975 bear striking similarities with Trinidadian African-Creole expressions (1979:107):

Yoruba	Trinidadian Africa-English Creole
Emi lo mbu?	Is me you 'busing?
mo bu e niyen. Kilo fe se fun.	Yes, I wish you self. What you
Mi? Iya aje!	have with me. You witch!
Maa kuku f'ejo e sun iya e na!	I footee report you to your mother, nuh.
E gbo iya were yi t'o mbu iya mi!	Hear this mad woman 'busing my mother!
Oro lo fe gbo. O o si by'oro naa.	Is commess you want hear? You don't hear commes
S'o ye e?	yet! You hear!
B'o o ba soro naa fun mi, nwon	You 'fraid. You can't tangle with me. You born
o bi daa!	bad/You bastard!
Oro e o jo mi loju! Abi baba repete!	Your language don't shock no body. Fat man!
Itan e ree lowo wa yi!.	Everybody know your business.
Kil'o so? O o ri p'ori e o pe!	What you saying? You don't see your head not
Ori temi pe daadaa!	good?
Iwo, tun lu mi k'a woo!	My head is quite normal.
	You, you beat me again and you see!

The following are idioms used in the Caribbean that reflect an African world-view (www.scholars.nus.edu):

Cut-eye
Hard ears
Suck teeth
You do well!
Let your hand drop
Got to call somebody aunt/uncle
Pick up your feet/heels and run
Run your mouth

In African-French Creole/Kweyol, the following examples can be heard (www.scholars.nus.edu):

koupé zié	[to] cut [your] eye [at somebody]
lafen ka tjenbé mwen	hunger holds me
ou ni djèl-kabwit	you have a goat-mouth
zié-yo fè kat	their eyes make four
zòwèy-li wèd	his ears [are] hard

Joseph Holloway provides us with these two examples from Caribbean African-English Creoles (www.slaveryinamerica.org):

"big eye" stems from Igbo, *anya uku*, meaning covetous, greedy.

"bogus" means deceit or fraud. It is similar to the Craibbean African-English Creoles *bo*, *ba*, the Hausa words *boko*, *boko-boko*, and Sierra Leonean Krio *bogo-bogo*, and the Louisiana African-French Creole *bogue*.

The following African idiomatic expressions are popular in the Bahamas (www.bahamas.com):

"day clean" and "first crow" refer to daybreak.

And the following African idiomatic expression is from Saint Croix (www.edu-cyberg.com):

If yo' put yo' ear a mango root yo' will hear crab cough. If you have patience and listen that close, you are bound to learn things.

African Linguistic Impact on Caribbean Literature

In her examination of the African impact on Caribbean literature, Maureen Warner Lewis delineates eight ways the impact has been manifested. She provides a plethora of literary examples from a variety of ALVs in her discussion. For the sake of brevity, only the descriptions of the eight ways are presented in the following paragraphs. The literary examples have been left out.

(1) Literary Use of Creole

The African legacy of word, idiom, pace and syntax has made it imperative that once the artist operates in Creole, the African influence is inevitable. Given that Creole is the mother tongue of the majority of the people in the Caribbean, oral literature is articulated predominantly in the basilect or the mesolect. As Lewis points out,

> The nationalistic winds of change in the 1940s gave an impetus to the use of Creole in novelistic and dramatic dialogue. But Claude McKay (Jamaica) was already a pioneer in Creole poetry, having since the 1900s written of Jamaican peasant life in *Songs of Jamaica* and *Constab Ballads*. His work was an inspiration to Louise Bennett (Jamaica) who began public performances of her artistic pieces in the 1940s. Onomatopoeia and reduplication are some of Bennett's techniques which derive from a peasant, and by extension, African, source. Only Samuel Selvon (Trinidad), however, has dared to write entire novels in the Creole medium. Timothy Callendar (Barbados) has followed

> this lead, but in the short story genre. Vic Reid (Jamaica) used a modified Creole in his *New Day* (1949). Derek Walcott (St. Lucia), playwright and poet, began using French Creole in his plays from the 1940s, and in his collection of poetry, *Sea Grapes* (1976), he used French Creole verse for the first time. Edward Brathwaite (Barbados) explored the dramatic dialogue potential of Creole in some of the poems in both *Rights of Passage* (1967), and *Islands* (1969). The enthusiastic reception of these pieces has inspired younger poets in the English-speaking Caribbean to use the modified Creole and urban ghetto language as their poetic medium. The immediacy of the vernacular and its strong dramatic urgency enhance the message in this form of poetry which is mainly of a protesting, rebellious, or critical nature (1979:108).

Indeed, many works with literary use of Creoles have been produced by Caribbean literalists since Lewis' observation.

(2) African Literary Devices in Caribbean Literature

According to Lewis, for reasons of ethnocultural continuity, Africa figures prominently in the oral traditions of the English-speaking Caribbean. These traditions, she posits, share forms, techniques, motifs, and archetypes with the universal imaginative experience of peasant peoples. She also suggests that "the predominantly African people of the Caribbean absorbed other prevailing cultural influences during the long period of European colonialism, and their thought and expression were especially influenced by their metropolitan mother tongue and, in the English Antilles, the King James Bible. Of lesser impact were the literary traditions derived from India, China and pre-Columbia America. Since the folklore and literary structures of all these matrices exhibit common features, these influences have served to reinforce the basic inherited traditions from Africa" (1979:108). Therefore, Lewis concludes, the "emphasis on the African impact ... is not intended as an assertion of its exclusivity, but merely for purposes of an examination of some areas of correspondence between English Caribbean verbal expression and that deriving from a major cultural input area across the Atlantic" (1979:208-9).

(3) Rhythmic Phrasing; Word Music; Word Play

Here, Lewis notes the phrasal expansion and repetition, close rhyme and rhythmic pulse, juggling of sound and meaning in Caribbean poetry, music and Rastafarian speech that are reminiscent of African poetic art. These poetic devices, she adds, have a great aural appeal and set the course towards closer identification between poet and people, poetry and folk speech (1979:109-112).

(4) Verbal Flamboyance—the Boast

Lewis tells us that the calypso (originally *kaiso*) is a direct descendant of several song types that are still prevalent in West Africa. The moralistic calypso is related to the *opala* music of the Yoruba, just to name one example. In this kind of calypso, didacticism is vital than melodic and rhythmic appeal. The narrative/ humorous/ironic calyso displays verbal or situational wit, exposes topical scandals, satirizes, or heaps merciless invective on the object of scorn. This latter type of calypso necessarily involves the motif of the boast and self-adulation, whereby the singer is brave, fearless, and invincible (1979:112).

Lewis finds similarities between the invective/boast *kaiso* genre of the traditional masquerades of Trinidad Carnival "robber talk" and Chinua Achebe's *Arrow of God*. This is the language of confrontation that had its strongest cultural manifestation in 19th and early 20th Centuries Trinidad in the *kalinda* or *bois-stick* fight. Stick-fighting bands were each accompanied by their chantwell (*chanterelle*) or cheerleaders who hurled defiance at the opponents of their patrons. Lewis also finds similarities between the theme, motifs and verbal formulae of the *kalinda* songs and those of a Yoruba *ijala* or hunter's songs (1979:112).

(5) Proverbs

The proverb, animal tales, tales of the supernatural, historical legends and creation myths are among the spoken oral literary forms in the Caribbean. Due to its topography that allows far-flung relatively isolated settlements, Jamaica has retained more proverbs in its basilect and mesolect compared to Trinidad. Proverbs reflect the distillation of the wisdom peasants glean through alert observation of their surroundings. They also tend to encapsulate a narrative. Evident in the kernel and expanded narrative is a communal imperative, a closeness to nature. The Caribbean proverb, just like that on the African continent, is sensuous and "alive" (Lewis, 1979:115).

(6) The Saga

Caribbean writers have utilized the historical legend in highly structured prose. They have recalled the indomitable courage and love of liberty displayed by their antecedents in the land—the Native Americans: confronted with subjugation by the conquering Spaniards, they hurled themselves *en masse* over the rocky sea-cliffs and into the Caribbean Sea. This historic narrative was retold by the younger generation at the time of the islands' struggle to gain independence from colonialists, serving as an essential beacon guiding the actions and attitudes of the islands' future leaders. Apart from the ethnic epic in prose, Caribbean writers also feature several personal histories that serve as means employed by folk speech to point to social manners, the communal or individual ethos, and the tension within society. They use the saga to such dimensions and with such resonance that certain characters take on mythological significance (Lewis, 1979:115-6).

(7) Allegory: The Dream Vision

According to Lewis, while the allegorical narrative has made only limited impact on written Caribbean literature, folk imagination still works and expresses itself strongly in terms of symbols that are largely apprehended in dreams and visions. The 1992 Nobel Laureate, Derek Walcott, has used elaborate fantasy of a dream to explore the tortured and ambivalent attitudes toward color and ethnicity in Caribbean society. Guyana's Wilson Harris often made use of revelation by dream to arouse the consciousness of his "characters." Allegory is also a favorite device of the *kaiso*, particularly, albeit not exclusively, when delicacy of presentation is imperative. The *kaiso* audience may be fascinated by a calypso expressed in double entendre, but it may reject an overtly lewd calypso. These symbolic elements can be found in the shape, gesture, and language of religious and secular rituals of the largely African-derived folklore (1979:116-8).

(8) Folk Narrative

The Akan Anansi is alive and well as a symbol of *samfie*—conmanship—in the Caribbean. The storytelling art continues to be revived in novels, on record and radio through theatrical performances. The repetition and interlocking cumulative structure of the Caribbean folk narrative, akin to *aro* in Yoruba, lends interest, rhythm, and symmetry to such work.

The Historical Approach

The African influence on Caribbean literature has also been examined in a historical framework. This approach encompasses four eras: (1) from the 16th Century to mid-19th Century, (2) the first 30 years during colonial rule (1930s), (3) the years just prior to independence between the 1940s and 1960s or pre-independence Renaissance, and (4) the period after independence.

From the 16th to the 19th Century, autobiography and poetry were the most prevalent literary works created by African Caribbeans. These works introduced themes that became common in Caribbean literature: displacement, exile, migration, and questions of identity. The history of Mary Prince, an enslaved West

Indian (related by herself), emerged as the most prominent of these writings in English. Early Caribbean writings in Spanish witnessed that of the biography of the enslaved African Juan Francisco Manzano of Cuba in the 1820s and 1830s, Jose Maria Herida Placido (an enslaved African who was executed in 1844 for his role in a slave uprising) and the African Cuban anthropologist Miguel Barnet. Max Urena of the Dominican Republic produced nationalist works in the 19th Century. The French-speaking Caribbean saw works by Emeric Bergeaud and Desmevar Delorme (www.welcometothecaribbean.com).

Distinct national literary traditions emerged in the 20th Century, as a few Caribbean countries were able to throw off the yolk of colonialism. During the fledgling years of the 1930s, a movement celebrating African culture and values rose to prominence. The movement was organized in France and named *Negritude*. Its founders, however, included Leon Gontram Damas of French Guiana and Aimé Césaire of Martinique. René Maran of Martinique won the Prix Goncourt (a French literary prize) with the novel, *Batoula* (1921), which called for identification with Black culture. In the Spanish-speaking Caribbean, African themes were present in a most exotic manner, depicting African and Black identity for artistic inspiration. Prominent writers in this movement included Luis Pales Matos of Puerto Rico and Emillo Ballagas of Cuba. The works of Cuban poet Nicolás Guillén from the 1930s shared sentiments with the politics of *Negritude* and addressed issues surrounding the struggle against colonialism. Cuba's Alejo Carpentier achieved recognition with his novels in which he explores the history and sources of Caribbean culture. The English-speaking Caribbean gave rise to prominent writers including Jamaican novelist Tom Redcam (Thomas Macdermot), Jamaican poet Claude Mckay, who emerged as the best known internationally. Mckay later became one of the leading writers of the Harlem Renaissance, the flowering Black culture in New York in the 1920s and 1930s. Other prominent writers included C. L. R. James of Trinidad, whose works protested against colonialism and helped to define the anti-colonial political and cultural struggles of his time. He was also instrumental in the formation of the literary magazines *Trinidad* founded in 1929 and the *Beacon* founded in 1931; these publications were pivotal in the development of a Caribbean literary tradition. Alfred Mendes and Ralph de Boisiere (Trinidadians) contributed articles and poetry to these magazines (www.welcometothecaribbean.com).

The pre-independence Renaissance period witnessed the emergence of a generation of writers whose works called for liberation and presented a distinctive portrait of Caribbean culture. Jamaica's Vic Reid looked forward to a "new day" of independence in his 1949 novel appropriately titled *New Day*; Roger Mais also of Jamaica employed Jazz rhythms in his poetic language to portray the displaced, downtrodden, urban population of the Caribbean in his work. Another Jamaican, Una Mason, did similar work using Blues rhythm in her collections of poetry. A vivid portrait of Guyana's countryside and society was presented by Edgar Mittleholzer in his 1950 novel, *A Morning At The Office*. One of the first and most important works dealing with childhood and coming of age in a colonial setting was the 1953 novel, *In The Castle Of My Skin*, by Barbados' George Laming. It is a novel about the struggles of three young boys with poverty, a colonial education, social change and the forging of an identity; in the background is the promise of migration to the metropolitan centers. The mythology of Africans and Native Americans was emphasized in Wilson Harris' 1960 novel, *Palace of the Peacock*, while Martin Carter's *Poems of Resistance* sought liberation from colonialism. This period also saw a number of active female writers. Guyana's Beryl Gilroy wrote novels, children's stories, and an autobiography. Jamaica's Sylvia Wynter incorporated elements of folk culture into her work. Dominica's Phyllis Shand Allfrey won recognition for her analysis of colonial power in her work, and Jean Rhys received critical acclaim for her novels about women caught in situations they were unable to change (www.wlecometothecaribbean.com).

The post-independence period saw the emergence of poets from the English-speaking Caribbean; Nobel Laureate Derek Walcott from Saint Lucia is perhaps the best-known Caribbean writer internationally. In addition to his poetry, he is also known as a playwright. At the same time, Eduard Kamau Brathwaite was challenging the formal structures of European poetry by adopting the rhythms, references and language of the African and African Caribbean traditions. Brathwaite broadened the possible use of language in his works for many subsequent writers, including Jamaican oral poets Mutabaruka, Linton Quesi Johnson, and John Binta Breeze. Earl Lovelace is among the noted English-language writers born in Trinidad and Tobago. His works on issues of poverty, education, and village life won a Commonwealth prize. The French-speaking Caribbean saw prominent writers in Guadeloupe's Daniel Maxim and Martinique's Edouard Glisant and Patrick Chamoiseau. Chamoiseau explored issues of Black identity and Creole cultural identity. The latter was produced in collaboration with Jean Bernabe and Rafael Confiant. Chamoiseau's 1929 novel, *Texaco*, won the Pri Goncourt. Female writers also became quite noted. Maryse Conde of Guadelopue is today considered a significant voice among the writers of the period, having won several French prizes for her works. Simone Schwarz-Bart also of Guadeloupe wrote about the search for identity. Nancy Morejon of Cuba is still recognized as a leading poetic voice. Her collection entitled *Cuaderno de Granada 1984* (*Grenada*

Notebook 1984) honors participants of Grenada's socialist revolution in 1983 (www.wlcometothecaribbean.com).

Indeed, Caribbean writers have impacted the international arena and have gained worldwide recognition for their numerous works. Embedded in these works are the traditions of storytelling that originated out of Africa and in supernatural tales from African religions. Proverbs, riddles and sayings that reinterpret African traditions are also most prominent in Caribbean literature.

Ausbau and *Abstand* Considerations

As Ralph Fasold (2003), my former professor of linguistics and long-time scholar of African American English, recounts in his 2003 North West Center of Linguistics Annual Lecture, it is common for linguistics textbooks to maintain that the concepts "a language" and "a dialect" are not exclusively linguistic notions, but also involve political and social factors. Put differently, the distinction between what should be called a language or a dialect cannot be made on linguistic criteria alone, particularly on the basis of the common-sense criterion "mutual intelligibility." For example, a linguistics textbook written by Fromkin, Rodman and Hyams (2002) that is widely-used in the United States confesses that "Because neither mutual intelligibility nor the existence of political boundaries is decisive, it is not surprising that a clear-cut distinction between language and dialects has evaded linguistics scholars" (2002:446). In a similar vein, Peter Trudgill's popular textbook, *Sociolinguics: An Introduction to Language and Society*, admits that "The criterion of 'mutual intelligibility', and other purely linguistic criteria, are, therefore, of less importance in the use of the terms *language* and *dialect* that are political and social and cultural factors ..." (1995:4). Nevertheless, regardless of how evasive or of less importance linguistic criteria are, most of the linguistics literature seems to suggest that linguistic criteria are crucial. Stated in another way, ultimately, the decision about what is a language and what is a dialect cannot be determined without linguistic expertise.

The crucial issue is whether or not one thinks it is possible that languages can be natural objects discoverable by employing methods of the natural sciences. If one thinks that there is no such possibility because *everything* is ultimately a social construct, then s/he will think that the point is too self-evident to be debated. Fasold's contention is that while it is conceivable that languages might be scientifically-discoverable natural objects, but in fact they are not. Ulrich Ammon (1989:31ff.) explicitly rejects this conclusion. Ammon argues that a political scientist would not accept a political system as a democracy just because its population calls it that, nor would a biologist consider an eel a snake because people consider it one. The difference is that political scientists and biologists can establish criteria by which democracies can be distinguished from other kinds of political systems, and biologists can tell one how to define snakes so as to exclude eels. Linguists, not for lack of effort, have been unable to determine criteria by which languages can be distinguished from dialects or other kinds of linguistic systems.

Ausbau and Abstand Languages

The problem of socio-political versus linguistic influences on assigning language or dialect status has been taken up by Heinz Kloss. He distinguishes between what he termed *Ausbau* and *Abstand* languages. An abstand language, a "language by distance," according to Kloss, is one that is so different from other related grammars that "a linguist would have to call it a language even if not a single word has ever been written in it" (1967:29). He is convinced that abstand language is "predominantly" a linguistic concept and "assume[s] that linguists are in a position to apply final, reliable and uniform criteria" on establishing status as languages for abstand languages (1967:30). Fasold argues that no such criteria exist or are likely to be disovered. In practice, then, according to Fasold, Kloss's notion is taken to mean that an abstand language is so distinct in linguistic properties from any language with which it might be associated that it would be obvious to any linguist that there exists a language and not a dialect.

Kloss's concept of "ausbau language," a "langauage by expansion," on the other hand, is fundamentally socio-political: i.e. ausbau languages have been deliberately reshaped to allow a wide range of literary expression. Fasold's own view is that elaboration for purposes of literary expression and the like is a rigid criterion. For Fasold, a language is a language if it has been socially constructed. If a social group exists that believes and acts as if a linguistic system is a language, then it is one.

Trudgill discusses the fate of the status of languages, depending, as he views it, on a combination of their abstand-ausbau properties and their socio-political circumstances. Trudgill emphasizes the fact that abstand is a relative concept and one can speak of degrees of abstand. The languages he refers to as *absolute* abstand languages—those, like Basque, that have no related languages anywhere—are, he believes, guaranteed status as separate languages regardless of the social setting. Of Basque, for example, Trudgill argues that "There is no possibility of claiming that it might be a dialect of some other language" (1992:168).

According to Fasold, other linguistic systems are part of dialect continua such as the West Germanic, West Romance, and North and South Slavic continua in Europe or, one might add, any number of similar continua elsewhere, like the

Nguni and Sotho languages of South Africa, the Mayan languages of Mexico and Guatemala, and continua of Aryan languages in India. Whether these systems are considered languages or dialects, for Fasold, depends on social construction, with or without ausbau. Since this is the case, Fasold argues that status as a "language" can be created and dismantled over time.

For Fasold, returning to the question of whether or not languages are natural objects to be discovered by science, it seems clear to him that if the answer is yes, then the notion "ausbau language" is the oxymoron. He reasons that if there is such an object as a language, independent of its social construction, then one can no more make a dialect a language than s/he can make an eel into a snake by giving it a suit made of scales and letting it wiggle on the ground. He adds that if there is no such natural object, but language always and in every case must be socially constructed, then "abstand language" takes on the relatively trivial meaning, language so different from other surrounding linguistic systems that people are unlikely to construct it as a part of another language. Abstand then, he concludes, becomes ultimately a study of people's perceptions of difference.

Social Construction of African Language Varieties in the Caribbean

In the Caribbean, the debate about whether or not ALVs are languages in their own right continues. On one side of the argument, European language purists call ALVs "lazy languages" and dismiss them as "vernaculars." On the other side of the debate, supporters of ALVs say that they are languages in their own right because they differ from the European languages in their phonetic and grammatical systems—the measures of what make a language distinct (www.educyberg.com). In addition, ALVs have their own "standards," have communities of speakers, are capable of expressing in writing any concept that can be expressed in European or any other languages, and certainly can be expressed orthographically in uniform ways that can—and should—encourage literacy development (www.jamaicans.com).

In Haiti, for example, there is an argument going on about whether its African-French Creole/Kweyol should have become the official language of the country when independence was declared in 1804. While to this day an overwhelming majority of Haitians speaks Creole and no French at all, many still see Creole as being inferior. Since Creole is the most widely spoken language, it is imperative that it be employed in schools and public facilities. When French is used in Schools and in public facilities, it is employed as a form of power against those who do not speak the language. The use of French as the only language of education also limits education to the majority of the Haitians who cannot speak it. This has resulted in a significant illiteracy rate (Lherisson, 2000).

Most frustrating for linguists is the futility of their efforts to construct ALVs as structured linguistic systems, and thereby to break the subtle and destructive iconization of their speakers. A large part of this futility seems to stem from sharp differences between the everyday use of the terms "dialect" and "standard" and the linguists' use of the same terms. When ALVs are defended as systematic and well-ordered dialects, they are inevitably contrasted with "standard" European languages. But the term "standard" is of two types: *minimum standards* and *arbitrary standards*. Minimum standards are specifications that must be met or exceeded for acceptability. Safety standards for automobiles are an example. If an automobile lacks the right features and properties of structural integrity, it may fail the standards and the manufacturer may not be able to sell it. In essence, minimum standards are imperative for an item to be considered "good enough." When minimum standards are lacking, the item has failed and should not be put into use.

Arbitrary standards are of a different sort. An example provided by Fasold is that the United States uses Fahrenheit degrees in measuring temperatures, including ambient air temperatures in weather reports. Most of the world measures temperatures in degrees Celsius. Fahrenheit degrees are harder to use and interpret and are based on less sensible criteria than Celsius degrees are and that the Fahrenheit system is, hence, inferior. However that may be, Fahrenheit degrees serve an important function as an agreed-upon arbitrary standard that people in the United States have come to understand and use. It is not imperative that the best system of temperature measurement is employed, as it is that all Americans agree on the same—arbitrary—standard.

When linguists employ the term "standard language," they invariably and implicitly mean an *arbitrary* standard. There are advantages to have an agreement on certain arbitrary standards for some language uses. In European languages, there are general tacit agreements on what these standards are. The standard language may not be the best possible constellation of linguistic features available; in fact, Fasold has demonstrated elsewhere that in some ways (for example, in making distinctions among kinds and times of actions and states), standard English is demonstrably inferior to Ebonics. But just as there is general agreement in favor of the Fahrenheit standard, even if the Celsius standard is probably better, the arbitrary standards that have been agreed upon for European languages are unlikely to be abandoned any time soon. It is general social acceptance that gives a workable arbitrary standard, not the inherent superiority of the item it specifies.

Fasold observes that in general conversation about language standards, however, the assumption made by the vast majority of people, who have not studied the nature of language in depth, is that the term "standard language" refers to *minimum* standards. If there is any variation from what is understood to the language standards, it is not seen as adherence to an alternative set of standards, but as a failure to achieve acceptable quality. Just like the house that fails to meet the building code standards, or an automobile that does not meet safety standards, nonstandard language is considered unfit to be used. The users of these dialects must, based on this view, be brought up to the minimum standard, for their own good as well as for the good of the society in general. In such a context, it seems the oxymoron to speak of ALV in the Caribbean or any variety other than standard European languages as "rule-governed." If a language fails to meet minimum standards, it has *io ipso* failed to be governed by the only rules that count. It is impossible to hold the minimum standards view of standard European languages and still believe that nonstandard varieties are rule-governed. A variety may either be ruled-governed or it may be nonstandard. It cannot, for most people, be both. When linguists assert that nonstandard varieties are rule-governed, although nonstandard, the perceived contradiction prevents us from making sense, or from being taken seriously.

At the height of the Oakland school board Ebonics debate, I was interviewed on the German International Radio, with offices located at 3132 M Street, NW in the heart of Georgetown in Washington, DC, on January 15, 1997. During the interview with the two hosts, a male and a female, it was obvious that they considered Ebonics not to meet the standards to which everyone in America rises up, but rather an instance of being lazy and going the other way.

Another view of the same problem involves the term "dialect." For linguists, dialects are speech varieties that make up a language, somewhat the way the slices make up the pie. One of these "slices" often achieves the status as a standard. But for the linguist, of course, this is an arbitrary standard. Given a different social history, one of the other dialects might have become the standard just as well.

For ordinary people, though, the term "dialect" and its relationship to the notion "language" is totally different. A "dialect" is either a speech system that is to be used by people who are considered primitive and that do not quite make it as a language (e.g., "the dialects of the indigenous people of the Amazon jungle"—note that they have "jungles" while we in the United States have "forests"), or it is a perhaps quaint but surely faulty way of speaking a "language." In that sense, it is comparable to slips of the tongue, slang-laced conversation, excessive use of profanity and other perceived abuses of language. The linguist's view, as to be expected, is quite different.

Let us imagine what happens when a linguist says that an ALV in the Caribbean is a dialect that is orderly and rule-governed and worthy of respect. The term "dialect" fits into the folk taxonomy for the audience while the linguist is working with the linguistic taxonomy. The linguist thinks s/he has made a simple-to-understand statement that ought to be accepted on his/her authority as an expert on language. The statement is that the dialect ALV is one of a number of equally orderly dialects of a European language, including the standard one. The lay person, though, hears the word "dialect" and interprets it in terms of his/her taxonomy. Since dialects are presupposed to be corruptions of language, the claim that an ALV in the Caribbean is orderly and rule-governed cannot make sense, unless it means that this particular way of corrupting the language has certain characteristics that can be described systematically. They may even agree that speakers of the dialect are worthy of respect. After all, one would not judge someone too harshly for the occasional slip of the tongue, so s/he should not be too hard on someone who speaks a dialect once in a while. But the linguist's analysis will make no dent in the ordinary person's conviction that anyone who is able to speak only a dialect is in serious trouble. Such speakers have an immediate need to replace the dialect with the real language, perhaps being allowed to slip back into that particular kind of sloppiness in a few relaxed and casual settings, once the language is mastered. But the ordinary individual will never hear that the linguist is actually saying that the dialect of an ALV in the Caribbean is on a par with the standardized dialect and, given different historical developments, might even have *been* the standard.

An exchange between the hosts and I during the same radio talk show mentioned earlier shows that they implicitly held folk taxonomy and that I became caught in the no man's land between the linguistic and folk taxonomic understandings of the term "dialect." My only salvation was my making an analogy to Plattsdeutsches spoken in Switzerland and parts of Germany.

As Fasold points out, given the yawning chasm between linguistic and folk ideas of "standard" and "dialect," for linguists to convince the general public about our construction of an ALV while using terms like "standard European language" and "ALV dialect" starts us off immediately with a double handicap. Somehow, Fasold suggests, linguists have to dislodge the idea of minimum standards as applied to language and replace it with the alien concept arbitrary standards. At the same time, linguists have to redefine "dialect" from a kind of corruption of the real language to a notion of dialect as a legitimate component of language relevant at a particular level of analysis. This done, linguists have to persuade listeners that, by the way, an ALV is one of these co-dialects of a European language which may deviate from the arbitrary standards imposed on English while conforming to standards of its own. Fasold concedes that the likelihood of accomplishing all this is quite small, in spite of the fact that ALVs do have all the grammatical intricacies and capacity to make subtle grammatical distinctions that all language systems do and in some respects are able to make distinctions far more subtle than those which are possible in standard European languages. So far, as Fasold again concedes, this is the easier part of the argument—demonstrating that linguistic systems that are very close together may or may not achieve status as a separate language depending entirely on ideological considerations.

Abstand Dialects

For Fasold, this second part of the argument is more difficult, as the question is whether or not it would be possible to construct linguistic systems with substantial abstand as dialects of the *same* language. The most often-cited case like this is Chinese, where many language systems that are so different from one another as to make them virtually mutually unintelligible are constructed as dialects of the Chinese language. In this case, though, the "dialects" are clearly related to each other, historically and in general structure. Presumably, the Chinese dialects fall short of what Trudgill calls "absolute Abstand," on the basis of which two languages can never be considered co-dialects, no matter what ideology might be served by doing so. A crucial problem with the notion "absolute abstand," of course, is the criteria by which it can be recognized—criteria which have never been proposed. But to explore this issue more closely, it makes sense to consider whether any language systems with abstand so great that it might be taken as absolute have ever been constructed as dialects of the same language. Fasold, thinks that the answer is perhaps so.

African Language Varieties in the Caribbean as Languages of Abstand Dialects

As Fasold observes, a striking case in which language systems with substantial abstand may have been constructed as a single language involves another construction of Ebonics. The social construction of Ebonics is very much different from the construction of African American English or United States Ebonics. Ebonics is a language, or perhaps a family of languages, that unifies the people in the African Diaspora, and is separate from the European languages with which it (or they) share most of the vocabulary and with which they may be mutually intelligible. This concept of Ebonics has been developed by scholars in the Africancentric tradition. It is motivated by what they perceive as an attempt by European thinking to attribute most aspects of the history and culture of people of African descent outside of Africa to Western sources, thereby denying the agency of African people in these matters, and obscuring the unity of the people of the African Diaspora over against the people of European origin among whom they live. The response is to propose that the language system spoken by people of African descent in the Diaspora comprises a common language of African origin that is not to be mistaken for a variety of some European language such as English or French.

To comprehend this argument more clearly, Fasold suggests that one needs to look more closely at what might count as abstand. Some languages can have considerable lexical and phonological similarity with one language while displaying syntactic similarity to another. The case of Moldovian calqued on Russian is an example.

It is on the basis of the assumption that language relationships are determined on the basis of syntactic and not on the basis of lexicon that Africancentric scholars have argued for the unity of Ebonics and its distinction from English or any other European language. The position is explicitly articulated by Smith as follows:

> The fact is when one analyzes the grammars of the so-called "black English" dialect and the English spoken by the Europeans and Euro-Americans, the grammars are not the same. While there has been extensive borrowing or adoption of English and other European words, the grammar of the descendants of Niger-Congo African slaves follows the grammar rules of the Niger-Congo African languages ... In other words, based on a criterion of continuity in the rules of grammar, there is no empirical evidence that "Black English" ever existed (1996:52).

Smith is arguing that Ebonics is a separate language from English, despite the frequency of words from the lexicon of English and other European languages on the same grounds that one might argue that some Moldovian constructions are really Russian—since the underlying grammatical structure, not vocabulary, is what counts for computing abstand

Not only do Africancentric linguists construct Ebonics as distinct from English, they also intend Ebonics to include other linguistic systems spoken by descendants of Africans. Blackshire-Belay (1996) is explicit on this point. She lists the following language systems as part and parcel of the Ebonics Continuum:

In North America

Termed *Louisiana French Creole*. Used in parts of eastern Louisiana, but diminishing in numbers of speakers.
Termed *Black English* or *African American English*. English-based varieties spoken throughout the United States in African American communities, both rural and urban, south and north, male and female, and spoken among all socioeconomic groups.

In South America

Termed *Brazilian Creole Portuguese*. Used by Brazilians of African ancestry in rural areas. This variety is spoken *in* Sao Paulo.
Termed *Lingua Gerâl*. A Tupi-Guarrani-based variety used in Brazil. Now losing ground to Portuguese.

In the Caribbean

Termed *Caribbean Creole English*. About 30 English-based varieties are found throughout the islands of the Caribbean, some represented by several varieties. The largest is the Ebonics spoken in Jamaica, with more than two million speakers.
Termed *Virgin Island Dutch Creole*. Widely used in the 19th Century, but now nearly extinct.

Blackshire-Belay includes English-, Dutch-, Portuguese-, French- and even Tupi-Guarani-lexified Creoles along with Ebonics as spoken in the United States within the Ebonics continuum. She asserts:

> The most fascinating characteristic about these so-called pidgins and Creoles is that despite the fact they display many obvious differences in sounds, grammar, and vocabulary, they have a remarkable amount in common. Ebonics contains structural remnants of certain African languages, although the vocabulary is overwhelmingly English, French, or Spanish. My position is that Ebonics is rooted in the African experience, on the basis of the linguistic evidence reflected in the system and comparable to the system within many of the African languages of the Niger-Congo family, that is Twi, Igbo, Ewe, Efik (1996:20).

Indeed, what Blackshire-Belay speaks of is a family tree of Ebonics. Similarly, Africologist Robert Twiggs (1973) in some places speaks of a Pan-African language in the Western Hemisphere as a language; in other places, he speaks of it as a language *system*. Following through on the position taken by Smith and apparently endorsed, at least in part, by Blackshire-Belay, Fasold suggests that there would be no reason not to take all the points on Blackshire-Belay's continuum as dialects of the same language. That is, if what counts is syntactic structure and not vocabulary, then a language lexified by French is the same language as a language lexified by English, as long as both are based on the same grammar.

Even more important is the fact that Africancentric scholars do not rest their case only on the supposed structural susbtrate from African languages, but also on thought patterns, gestures and other criteria beyond nuts-and-bolts linguistics. As Smith puts it,

> In the sense that Ebonics includes both the verbal and paralinguistic communications of African Amercan people, this means that Ebonics represents an underlying psychological thought process. Hence, the non-verbal sounds, cues, gestures, and so on that are systematically used in the process of communication by African American people are encompassed by the term as well (1996:54).

And Blackshire-Belay adds: "Nonverbal communication patterns in African culture, for example, rhetorical style, body movement, expressions, gestures, are included in the process" (1996:20 fn. 2).

Ebonics, then, can only be partially constructed by means of the Eurocentric standard practices of linguistics. And since Eurocentric linguistics has no privileged position in this regard, there is no reason why the construction of a language from such apparently absolute abstand varieties as United States Ebonics and African language varieties in the Caribean should not succeed.

The ideology that is being promoted by the construction of Ebonics as a language, or at least as a continuum of related languages, is not hard to discern. Focusing on the undeniable and continuing effects of slavery and present-day racism perpetrated by people of European origin, Africancentric scholars seek grounds on which all those of African origin who have had and are having this experience can be unified and at the same time separated from European-origin society. They are dismayed that so much of the lives and cultures of people who trace their origins to Africa is explained by Eurocentric scholarship as having ultimately European origins, even if perhaps shaped by their unique experiences as Africans. It then seems reasonable to look for origins for present-day cultural institutions in the African Diaspora in Africa, at a time when African people have the luxury of agency to develop their traditions without the interference of European oppressors. Ebonics the language, then, becomes iconic to all that unifies people of African origin as against Europe-based societies in which they live. In fact, these considerations are not so different from many of the cases of the construction of ausbau languages described in Kloss (1967) and Trudgill (1992), among others.

In essence, Africancentric scholars have satisfactorily constructed Ebonics as a language of abstand dialects. In fact, this construction of Ebonics briefly became part of official policy in one school district in one city in the United States, during the Oakland, California Ebonics debate of 1996 and 1997.

Conclusion: A Great and Creative Feat of Resistance

Under slavery, African languages were violently suppressed in the Caribbean just like in other parts of the Diaspora. Despite this, Africans in the Caribbean preserved the phonological, syntactic and grammatical core of their mother tongues. The African language varieties that emerged and survived in the Caribbean were the result of a great and creative feat of resistance, overt and covert.

From the 18th Century onwards, a handful of the estimated 100 million Africans who had been caught up in the Transatlantic slave trade and transported to the Americas began writing about their enslavement and the African societies they had left behind. The works of individuals such as James Albert Ukawsaw Gronniosaw, Ignatius Sancho, Ottobah Cugoano and Olaudah Equiano were among the first to attempt to present the Western world with a view of Africa that was not shrouded by racial prejudice or avarice. From the mid-19th Century up to the mid-20th Century, the torch was carried by scholars such as Edward Wilmot Blyden (Danish West Indies, known today as the United States Virgin Islands), Henry Sylvester Williams (Trinidad and Tobago), Marcus Garvey (Jamaica), C. L. R. James (Trinidad and Tobago), George Padmore (Trinidad and Tobago), Frantz Fanon (Martinique), Aime Cesaire (Martinique) and many others. In the works of these intellectual giants, African identity, culture and identification with the African Motherland figured prominently (Cobley, 2001).

Despite this great effort, the inauguration of African Studies as a formal academic discipline in the Caribbean had to await the era of decolonization. In 1948, the University College of the West Indies (UCWI) was established in Jamaica as one of the Asquith Colleges. UCWI's curriculum was devised largely in England, and its degrees were accredited by the University of London. However, just months after gaining its own charter as a degree-awarding institution in

1962, finally breaking the direct colonial link with Britain, UCWI took steps at the renamed University of the West Indies (UWI) to develop expertise in African History (Cobley, 2001).

In 1963, a young and brilliant Guyanese graduate of the UWI named Walter Rodney traveled from Jamaica to study for a doctorate in African History at the School of Oriental and African Studies (SOAS) in London, England. While at the SOAS, Rodney completed a doctoral dissertation entitled "A History of the Upper Guinean Coast, 1545-1800." After receiving his doctorate in 1966, his first teaching job was a temporary assignment at the University College of Dar es Salaam in Tanzania. After completing a year of teaching at Dar es Salaam, Rodney returned to Jamaica to take up a teaching position at UWI in October of 1967. At the same time that Rodney began to develop an academic program in African History, he also began speaking regularly at public events organized by the Rastafarians (then in ferment after the late Haile Selassie's visit to Jamaica in April of 1966) and many other Black consciousness groups. Rodney also gave a series of lectures on Black Power at the Student's Union on the Mona Campus. Since he was a member of the long intellectual tradition of the Black Atlantic, Rodney's training as an Africanist pitched him directly into the debates about Black identity that were raging at the time in Jamaica. The politically conservative Jamaican government became alarmed by the specter of a radical Black Power movement in the country. In October of 1968, while Rodney was attending the Black Writers' Conference in Montreal, Canada, the government took the opportunity to bar his re-entry into Jamaica. The move sparked riots in Jamaica. Rodney returned to Dar es Salaam, where he stayed until 1974. During this period, his famous book, *How Europe Underdeveloped Africa*, was published in 1972 by Bogle-L'Ouverture Publications in Britain (it was republished by Howard University Press in Washington, DC in 1974). His decision to return to the Caribbean in 1974 had been prompted by a job offer as Professor of African History at the University of Guyana. However, upon his arrival, he found that the authoritarian regime of Forbes Burnham had scuttled his appointment. Rodney stayed in Guyana to work as a member of the radical opposition to Burnham's dictatorial rule until he (i.e. Rodney) was assassinated by a car bomb in Georgetown, Guyana, in 1980 (Cobley, 2001).

In 1965, two other young graduates, Alvin Thompson and Winston McGowan, followed Rodney's footstep from UWI to SOAS. Thompson and McGowan returned to the Caribbean to take up teaching positions at the University of Guyana in 1969 and 1970, respectively. Thompson moved to Cave Hill Campus of the UWI in Barbados, where he was largely responsible for the development of the African History undergraduate program. Building on these foundations, by the end of the 1980s, the History Department at Cave Hill had hired three faculty members with expertise in African History (Cobley, 2001).

In addition to these developments in African History, Caribbean scholars in a variety of other disciplines began developing an interest in African linguistic, religious, creative and performing arts survivals in the Caribbean. Among the key figures in these developments were Edward Kamau Brathwaite, Mervyn Alleyne, Maureen Warner Lewis, and Rex Nettleford. A key vehicle for such studies was the African Studies Association of the West Indies (ASAWI) formed in Jamaica in 1967 (Rodney served briefly as its treasurer). Between 1967 and 1976, the ASAWI published the *Bulletin*, which later became the *Caribbean Journal of African Studies* (CJAS) in 1978, albeit it was short-lived. More enduring is the major in African Studies that was established at the UWI's Mona Campus in the 1970s. Among the more important projects begun during these years that sought to incorporate work on African-Caribbean connections was the Caribbean Lexicography Project at Cave Hill directed by Richard Allsopp (Cobley, 2001).

As nationalism intensified in the 20th Century, more attention was paid to African linguistic origins. The Haitian poet Jacques Roumain stressed the value of his African culture. Nicolas Guillén, one of Cuba's most eminent poets, wrote some of his best works as Black poetry based on the rhythms of African Cuban music. The novels, poetry, dance and mime of the Caribbean have all incorporated African speech patterns, styles, and concepts and have tried to express the spirit of the African cultural heritage. In the Nobel Prize-winning poetry of Derek Walcott and the autobiographical short stories of Jamaica Kincaid, an effort is made to reconcile the differences between the writers' African Caribbean and adoptive white milieus (Cruz, 2000:14).

4

Post-Colonial Pan-Africanisms and Caribbean Contributions: Behind Du Bois' Veil is Fanon's Muscle on a Herculodian Trip

Jim Perkinson

Introduction

Africa in our midst, that utterly alien Africa of roadside corpses, cruelty, and anarchy.

—Jared Taylor, editor, *American Renaissance* magazine, in reference to New Orleans after Katrina

Yale art historian Robert Farris Thompson, in a talk given at the African American Museum of Detroit on November 8, 1997, provocatively asserted that one of the unforeseeable results of the African slave trade was that now "the entire Western world rocks to an African beat." Updated for 21st Century permutations of the globalized trade in hip-hop culture, we could perhaps rejoin: "indeed, Robert, now the *entire planet* pops a socket to an African mock-up of the absurdity and vitality of being alive." Hip-hop culture today—the central cultural export of the most powerful nation-state on the planet deriving from its most marginalized community—is efflorescing around the globe as a youth-cult medium that is the closest thing yet seen to an international Esperanto. With a bit of poetic license we could perhaps even style this planetary development as the emergence of a long dormant ancestral commonality now claiming its day in the sun in social ecologies as divergent as Ghana and Greece, Russia in the east and Bahia in the south, Inuit communities in the artic and Hawaiian homes in the tropics, youthful gatherings in Katmandu and boutique clubs in *gai* Paris, Pakistani, Bengali and Iraqi contexts of struggle and all manner of Latino movements below southern borders. To what degree can such an evident and surprising code of the body be given analytical currency as an inchoate mode of "Pan-Africanism"—both for better and worse?

Bronx-Caribbean Reverberation

Hip-hop is only the latest Afro-heritage artifact to gain adherence across such a scale of difference as the entire Atlantic basin (jazz and blues, reggae and mambo, funk and techno, to name only a few, boast an attraction that is at the least diaspora-wide). Indeed, much of its early ambiance was established as a Caribbean confluence with New York influence, merging toast traditions from Jamaican dub with Puerto Rican "crazy legs" break-dance moves, Afro-Cuban conga-drum "improv" already alive and throbbing on South Bronx streets, and the funk beats and free-style feats and meat-shaking heat of James Brown, Sly and the Family Stone, and George Clinton. With his massive stereo system speakers named the "Herculords" rocking the block, Jamaican DJ Kool Herc's early 1970s heavy-amp yard parties transplanted Kingston outdoor celebration-style to South Bronx parks to launch the peculiar subterranean base-beat-bombastics characteristic of hip-hop animation (Rose, 1994:51; George, 1999:xi, 7). The gymnastic swipes and swirls, helicopter-chopping legs and head-spinning "drills" on hard concrete of groups like Rocky Steady Crew, Dynamic Rockers and New York City Breakers gave Nuyorican (New York Puerto Rican) prominence to b-boy and–girl battle-drama in break dancing's second phase from 1979 to 1982. Haitian-Puerto Rican *grafittero* Jean-Michel Basquiat helped propel "tagging" into a major political code of conflict enacted between disenfranchised street youth and city officials throughout the 1970s with his SAMO-signature claiming Manhattan walls for the call-response of poor artists with no access to either palate or gallery. Earliest "old school" definers of the culture (now Smithsonian hip-hop display consultants), Africa Bambaataa and Grandmaster Flash, both boast immediate families from Barbados, while the latter found himself in stiff competition, over "the whirling wheels of steel," with Puerto Rican Carlos Mandes, aka Charlie "Chase" (racing after Flash's sizzle-fingered fame with heat of his own). The accounting could easily go on at length to detail the five-culture (Barbados, Jamaican, Puerto Rican, Cuban, North American) conjunction that, according to Thompson, catapulted 1970s South Bronx hip-hop into an ever-growing national prominence as a form of Creole retort to the Bronx's dominant-culture dismissal as the archetypal scenario of Western urban apocalypse (given visual currency in popular films like *Fort Apache, Wolfen* and *Koyaamsqatsi*) (Thompson, 1996:213).

Hip-hop in its origins was never *not* a Caribbean-American gumbo on top of a New York flame. Nor, as it matured and morphed, did the creolized innovation on top of African American percussive insurgence or existential defiance cease. In the 1980s, as groups like Public Enemy, Boogie Down Productions, Brand Nubian, XCLAN, etc. began introducing a politicized focus on Black nationalism, "fading" Latino visibility in the process, Boriqua b-boys Ricardo "Puerto Rock" Rodriguez and Anthony "KT" (Krazy Taino) Boston, struck back in Splangish rhyme, remixing the times, combining Kangol caps and *cuchifrito* tastes, high-top sneakers and *piragua* vendors, giving rise, in their Latin Empire uptake of the Nuyorican poetic tradition of Miguel Pinero and Pedro Pietri, to successor *raperos* like Vico C, Ruben DJ, D-Squad, Lisa M, Brewsky MC and Queen Latina (Perkins, 1996:69-71). Later in the game, "Notorious" gangsta-rapper Biggie Smalls capitalized on his mother's Jamaican immigrant calypso-sensibility to develop a distinctively supple version of hard lyrical assault in his "beef" with West Coast rhymers, while Cypress Hill emerged as the largest-selling Latino flavor with its Cubano-Italiano squad. And at the contemporary end of the hip-hop quarter-century, Puerto Rican barrio boaster Daddy Yankee has emerged as San Juan signature of the latest rhyming revolution in the Caribbean remix of rap into a reggae-soca-hip-hop hybrid—storming ears north, south, east, and west—as the new club-craze known as *reggaetón*. In its "pot luck" caldera of beats and boasting (to mix metaphors like musics), hip-hop has long built on a diaspora-wide tradition of African-heritage syncopation with flavors Caribbean, European, and Latin American.

But hip-hop does stand relatively alone in exceeding merely black phenotypical allegiance as radically as it does, as the subject of ever-proliferating recombinatory practices with other cultural traditions, large and small, old and new, locally-maintained or globally-renamed (Perry, 2004:12-13, 20 & 24, Gilroy, 1993:28, 31). The news media clips noting the prevalence of prophetic rap riffs sounding out immigrant Muslim volatility in Parisian suburban *banlieues* ("ghettos")—for some years before the flames of 2005—is merely one more indication (Williams, 2005:A29). And obviously its spread is not an instance of mere "contagion" or quasi-evolutionary "mutation," but also capitalist propagation yielding profits and stupidity writ large. But it may also signal a deeper convolution.

Africa is mother of the planet—and perhaps of a certain shared predilection. Anthropological mapping of the migratory prehistory of the species back to the (so-called) "heart of darkenss" (Bynum, 1999:6, 14), genetic genealogies of population diversities tracing back to a tap root somewhere around Tanzania, neurobiologic recognition of the deep preconscious conditionality of all conscious activity (Bynum, 1999:81, 85-87, 93-95), epigenetic prescience about the role of repetition and rhythm in learning and memory—all conduce to the likely possibility of a species-wide affinity for a beat replete with the sounds—and sounding—of our common beginning. If the DNA bears witness to a shared genesis in blackness, why not also the deepest cultural codifications of our multiply-oriented articulations of desire! Is human yearning at core anchored in a memory of percussive vitality that to date finds its most complex expression and radical exploration in Afro-palpitations of identity? Robert Farris Thompson has traced the global efflorescence of what could be called "African percussive epistemologies" in not only musical, but visual, sartorial, plastic and philosophical modalities in *Flash of the Spirit*. Whether or not this intuition is mere post-colonial romancing of the stone-struck drum of ancestry, it is the idea that shall govern here.

At bottom the question that registers in this chapter is the unexplored ramifications of academically theorizing and politically embracing a genealogy that may well be as Afro-percussive in structure as it is Guinean in genesis. By this I mean to solicit not only a common biological origin but shared orientation towards rhythmic patterns that are Afro-centripetal in code and age. What such a thesis might mean if sustained in analysis remains a task for the future. Here I will rest content with merely outlining the possibility "archaeologically" and hinting at the stakes historically. It is crucial to assert upfront that I do not believe cultures anymore than genes are static and fixed for all time, nor that our labels of identification any more than our rituals of conditioning are essential to places or homogenized across groups. Having found ourselves already long diffused across the globe at the point in time (beginning in 1492) when we could readily navigate the world's waters with missions of venture and return, and vibrate its air with frequencies of sound and vision, it is clear that we now continually cross-propagate biologically and inter-digitate culturally and that such transactions are themselves part of the on-going colonial, neo-colonial and biocolonial history of this peculiarity of time we call modernity. But in the long process of coming to a new level of consciousness across the time of our trekking towards the utter extremities of the planet surface, a glaring contradiction continues to stab up into awareness out of the murk and miasma of our various mythologies of collective identity.

And that is that everywhere there lurk strange shards of memory of having once been dark in ancestry and African in originality and equally ubiquitous and strange mechanisms of repression of such a beginning. Edward Bynum's *The African Unconscious: Roots of Ancient Mysticism and Modern Psychology* gathers the cross-disciplinary evidence of the common ancestry and its psychogenetic epiphenomenality and underscores the artificiality of the will-to-forget that is so much in evidence around the globe (Bynum, 1999:76, 79). The evidence of the ancestry is too well established to bear repeating. The ubiquity of the repression underscored but left unexplained by Bynum goes to phenomena as different as the psychoanalytic evidence of the shadow figures that show up in dream-life across the globe and more historical obduracies like the caste-color system in India or the ancient Greek and Roman suppression of the Egyptian antecedents of European cultural achievements before and during the emergence of Christianity from Judaism.

The ruthlessness and seeming universality with which color gradation—where imbedded in social institution in history—articulates a value scheme privileging light over dark is both striking and refractory. It shows its bright symptom everywhere while its opaque etiology winds back into the mists of time and denial. Explanations have gone as "natural" as a species-preference for noon over midnight in ancient strategies to avoid becoming prey of large nocturnal hunters and as "social" as the illegitimate adaptation of Darwin to intraspecial notions of differentiation along the lines of race. But so far, the confession remains patent. No one really knows why the mysterious denigration gained purchase in memory and social order. Where we should be pouring a common libation to African ancestry across the entire globe, we shed blood, heap abuse and turn backs instead. Here the concern is not to venture a new reason, but to hover around the fact and let it "speak" a direction.

Sonic Pan-Africanism

That direction is towards a future planetary politics wrapped inside an immediately local pedagogy and grows out of my own location as a White male in various American contexts of education and activism. While inner city Detroit has been my own pedagogue of greatest power for more than 20 years—intervening in consciousness and body alike, tongue "tricked up" in triple-time rhyme at the podium or feet heated in base-beat on the dance floor—it is my new location in Denver, Colorado, among White students of privilege, taking ignorant umbrage at anything that discomfits their middle class pillage of the planet, that forms my locale of testing. I am currently conducting a course there called Shamanism, Racism and Hip-Hop Culture, the burden of which is to trick my clique of White-child tenants of the imperial dream into an alternative perception of the history they inhabit and the (hip-hop) tunes of terror and titillation they scavenge in blackface love at the local mall. That is to say, I try to use their fascination with machine-gun rhythm and booty-collisions on MTV to open up vision on how they got where they are. This might seem a far cry from the concern of the hour to re-imagine a Pan-African mission to halt predation of the home continent or exploitation of its diasporic labor forces, but today I don't think that anything less than a remaking of human "being" will be adequate to the problem. What summons to the idea of a planetary-wide revision of the place of Africa in international consciousness and practice is this evident attraction of an arguably "African" cultural code that is showing up like a rhizome under young skin around the globe (Gilroy, 1993:4, 28).

What qualifies something as African is, of course, part of the question. At the heart of the conviction offered here is an observation developed by Frantz Fanon about colonial Algerian resistance to French domination. The Martiniquean psychoanalyst divined the deep code of insurgence as one showing up in the release of muscular tension in rites of possession—a "canalizing of the impulse to murder" that Fanon lamented only in its squandering in ritual rather than in acts of political intentionality (Fanon, 1963:203, 220, 241, 291). This "deep reading" of the body under duress, disinterring a psychosomatic registry of suffering in the interests of mobilizing revolution, does not just stand as a tantalizing "what if," according to cultural critic Paul Gilroy. Rather, the cultural products of Black Atlantic communities of rhythm, using the body gathered in assembly as an instrumentality of memory, are themselves the repository of a potential resistance, a "banking" of energy awaiting its political ignition (Gilroy, 1987:75, 164 & 212, 1993:129, 198 & 212).

For Gilroy, the issue is not mere escape, but rather "conservation." Here the violence of domination, visited upon the colonized with an adventitiousness defying rationality, thwarting prediction and explanation alike, cannot be merely forgotten or disavowed (Long, 1986:9, 110 & 177). It is rather steeped, re-visited in antiphonal rituals that canalize the excess into a grammar of animation understood by the community (Barnes, 1997:xvi & xiii, Brown, 1984:198, Walker, 1972:104-115, Gilroy, 1993:200). Such is one meaning of possession cult activity in both diaspora and homeland alike. The percussive labor involved in re-dramatizing colonial pain articulates a form of political capital (Perkinson, 2001:567). It rekindles outrage precisely in the process of releasing umbrage and fear (Brown, 1997). Whether Black-church shout or Soweto stomp, vodu swoon or caboclo croon of possession, jazz jamboree melee, or Rasta reverie, the syncopated stylistics is more than just surface theatrics. The external form belies a muscular memory whose desperation is the very heart of self-consciousness. Of course, there is nothing automatic here. Fear can as easily paralyze and enervate as volatilize into a terrible epiphany. But it is also the recurrent witness of modern history that populations caught in the irresolvable dilemma of racialized forms of oppression, made to dwell without relief in a conscious "neither-nor," simultaneously demanded for labor and rejected for being, stand as a cipher for the rest of the human race.

What is irreducibly "African" in this scenario is not the experience of domination *per se,* but the function and historicity of racialization in the legitimation of such and the cultural resources brought to bear in on-going attempts to relativize the suffering imposed. "Africa" clearly marks the continent furthest out in the circuits of transnational capital today, the landmass most peripheralized in the course of the modern enterprise of plunder and pillage; "African" skin color and the various presuppositions of bestiality and backwardness it has been made to signify in the asymmetries of racialization likewise anchor the nether-most social position in global polities. The resulting consciousness, where the racial markers have been most viciously promulgated to police the boundaries of social inclusion, is perhaps most simply symbolized by something like Du Bois' double consciousness—a mode of mental meaning-making forced continuously to elaborate its self-references by way of its on-looking "White" other (Du Bois, 1993:16-17). Such hyper-conscious and vigilant probing of one's environment for the least signals of danger and tiniest apertures of opportunity has developed irony into a mode of embodiment, recurrently elaborated in cultural forms of expression, religious, political, and artistic, that compel fascination by their singular virtuosity (Gates, 1998:49, 54 & 71, Lattany, 1994:165-166). These "Black" cultural forms—promiscuously and unapologetically recombinant in poaching other cultural forms into the project of diasporic survival—are notoriously identifiable in their ever-proliferating hybridity (Hall, 1992:27-28, Gilroy, 1993:31).

What marks their appearance as "African" is the intensity of "the percussive"—a propensity to rework anguish into syncopated modalities of contrast, beauty into a sinuosity of embodied conflict, that in Thompson is described as "polyrhythm" and in hip-hop scholar Tricia Rose as "ruptured and layered flow" (Thompson, 1983:xiii-xvi. Rose, 1994:38-39). Nowhere on the face of the planet have cultures explored more exactingly and complexly the peculiar potencies of percussive epistemologies than in Africa. The propensity to articulate signs of reality in structures of sharpened contrast—whether in the medium of sound or vision, vocabularies of the body in motion or the tongue in recitation, hand on drumhead or fabric striped like a well-orchestrated riot—is not exclusively

Guinean, but *is* paradigmatically native to that mother continent. This cultural poetics of the "break," embroidering energy at the edge created by contrast, sharpens consciousness and heightens vitality by way of a vivacious tension (Baker, 1984:112, Perkinson, 2005:91, 95 & 101). Here is Spirit as "intensification"—not mere possession by what is dynamic, but a cultural predilection to probe the boundary where one thing abruptly meets its other.

Arguably, it is then this historic experience of irresolvable pain, locked and held in a social positioning of paradoxical inclusion/exclusion, remembered, explored, and transvalued in a poetics of percussive motion, that finds its latest incarnation in hip-hop beats commanding global attention. This is a "pan-africanism" written in the lower case not of script but base beat. But is it any less "African" for being a language of muscle on bone, a cognition refusing scission from either emotion or the body, showing itself symptomatic of internalized struggle and therapeutic in collective rituals eliciting planetary-wide responses on the part of the young? Indeed, what does such an attraction to percussion on such a scale, in fact, augur? How do we "read"? Or do we—who are so wedded to the order of more and more and better and better—just shake our heads and dismiss the effervescence as one more youthful excess?

Global N***a-fication

For Fanon, the "popping and locking" of Algerian ritual, simultaneously repeating and releasing the agony of colonial oppression, pointed to another possibility: he longed for it to be translated into revolutionary "murder" (Fanon, 1963:52-57). But even without that eventuation, the pain and its code offered an extant witness. It is a witness today going international in the emergence of what R. A. T. Judy calls "global n***a-dom" (from "nigga," the first word of which hereafter marked as "n***a" as distinct from "n***er").[1] Judy is actually paraphrasing the work of what he calls the hard core OG ("Original Gangsta"), Ice-T, on his 1991 Sire Records release, "Straight Up N***a" (Ice-T). Judy's treatment of the question of "n***a authenticity" in his article by that name in the Hip-Hop Studies Reader, *That's The Joint,* wrestles with the post-industrial modality of a "Blackness" now thoroughly commodified, packaged as "communicable affect," and

---

1.   As a white scholar treating this subject, my own discipline with respect to the word is never to speak it and refrain from writing it except for a single first time designation in any manuscript, in order thereby to mark what I judge to be the utter inappropriateness of white people ever using the word, on the one hand, but also to recognize the hotly contested reclamation and transvaluation of the word in altered form by certain segments of the Afro-diaspora world, on the other.

globalized across a wide range of cultures and social positions (Judy, 2004:107). That treatment seeks to think hip-hop at the crossroads of historic African American liberation struggles and the "moral malaise … of capitalism's contemporary hegemony over all aspects of life" (Judy, 2004:107).

Gone, argues Judy, is the safe haven of Black nurture of an earlier era, when it was still possible to separate society from economy, cultural movement from political domination, ghetto neighborhood from wider city, and identify clear champions of community morality, acting in the libratory tradition of the "bad-man" of blues fame (Judy, 2004:114). Rather, the new game is the reign of hypercommodification, penetrating society and folk community alike, rupturing morality "from within" Black neighborhoods in the agency of hard core rap itself. Emergent as the new social form of this hegemony—*the* dangerous identity *par excellence*—is the n***a, embodied quintessentially in the hard core gangsta rapper, perhaps most notoriously given political currency in the complex *persona* of a Tupac Shakur, probing and problematizing all technologies of governance, including those of the local Black community. This subject-position is outside the clear delineation of good from evil, morality from policing, authentic African American cultural form from its appropriation by transnational capital—a "commodity affect," paradoxically linking unique and unfungible experiences (of Blackness) with the possibility of a global appropriation of such in abstract and formulaic representations of anger, rage and pleasure (Judy, 2004:114). The shocking result, in Ice-T's words, is the "n***afication of even White suburban youth, among the varied adolescent constituencies constituting the range of rap's consumer-participants (Judy, 2004:113-114). But inside the easy appropriation, asserts Judy, is a constant expression of overflowing energy "pregnant with the future" (Judy, 2004:114). Adaptation to the force of commodification should not be confused with simple capitulation: transnational dilution of the product provokes hard-core reaction in efforts like Public Enemy's "Don't Believe the Hype." Inside the new pan-global possibility of "being a n***a" is the profound question of n***a *being*, according to Judy (Judy, 2004:113). The articulation of this difference is not a matter of separating out the morality of so-called "consciousness" (or "political") rap from the nihilism of hard core, but rather of ontology itself (Judy, 2004:115). At issue is human existence *writ large*. Is there life beyond the commodity *for any human being today?*

Judy's sharp refusal to let hard core hip-hop be dismissed as merely one more entertainment scheme in global capital's volatilization of experience in the marketplace pushes the inquiry here to its limit. The emergence of the transnational n***a—a site of mystification and interrogation gathering around its opaque gestures and insurgent attitudes and bumping beats a veritable menagerie of cultural backgrounds and youthful adherents—stands as a profound paradox in history that remains undeciphered ontologically and untapped politically. How did this precise incarnation of human nature become the touchstone of young vitality and reproduce its "language" across the planet? As I write, the northern suburbs of Paris literally "burn" with an immigrant outrage (at Western intolerance and dismissal) that by background is largely North African and Muslim, but by gestural semiotics of hands celebrating the flames emerging from exploding cars is clearly hip-hop in its defiance. How did the margins become the center? How did "Africa" become the signifier of olive and yellow and brown and red and yes, even white, adolescent aspiration?

Pan-Hip-hop-ification

In a world rendered almost instantaneous to itself in electronic digitalization, a confrontational bob of the head animated by a percussive strut of the feet is now everywhere extant. At core of the gestural code is the question of authenticity: "will the real n***a please stand up?" But as the OG has intimated—to an n***a everybody is an n***a (Ice-T, "Straight Up N***a"). How the human exists today among the post-modern tsunami of commodities is most sharply and paradoxically articulated by a ghetto body defying its captivity to the image ... from *within the image!* Hip-hop here functions as the Trojan horse of capital, delivering the enemy to the door of gated civility (Cf. Cuban "Negritude" painter Wilfredo Lam's similar conception of the hoped-for effect of his Surrealist paintings [Fouchet, 1976:188; Linsley, 2002:293]). The irony is inebriating. Historically, the commodification of Africans as chattel property in the Atlantic slave trade realized the quintessence of capital: a human body made over as laboring device, stripped of rights and all things human. Prior to this new modern "achievement" of thing-a-fication, the African had been proposed in European canons of correctness as "monstrously anomalous," "wildly hybrid," an *imago dei* operating theologically in reverse gear, but not yet mere object. The Curse of Ham mythology mobilized in medieval theology to comprehend Africanity charted a strange and mythic fall of ancient human being into near-faunal meaning—registering as dark skin growing out of a "Black" heart—and explained such as a matter of self-damnation issuing from bad choices (White, 1978:160-162; Bastide, 1970:272, 281). But the categories that projected that uncertain condition regarding eternal destination moved quickly into a significance of the subhuman as contact picked up after 1492 and, in short order, offered the Black body as mere commodity for the market. The Atlantic slave differed from the Aristotelian one in having its slave-status associated not only with an individualized condition of "bent back," but with a collective condition of curse appearing as color on the body-surface. Its exchange value was not only one of labor, but of a cautionary tale, in the economy of souls, that did serious theological work in leveraging whiteness as a presumption of spiritual "rightness" with God. That it is now, on the other side of this historical submergence of African significance in the commodity form, and of saved souls in a White body, a *Black* body that gestures brazenly from the midst of marketable objects as the postmodern and dystopian question of human being in its widest global signification is a remarkable bit of joker justice emerging from the trickster core of history's irrepressible underbelly. This is the zombie come back from the dead not only to labor for bread, but full of dread meaning in a red eyeball signaling comeuppance.

And that is precisely how hard core rap looks back at its corporate pimp from inside the market game: there is a flame of darkness there that remains unnamable and only uncertainly tamable in the commercial. It presumably (according to the stereotype) might just as readily fire a glock in the marketing man's face or put a penis in his fawning groupie daughter. But the mad poetics here should not be allowed to elide the philosophical glare of the opacity. This is also a question emerging like an unnamed gene from underneath White skin. Whose ancestor is this, really, who is now up inside the gated community in the leering grin of the transnational n***a? And whose code is throbbing the young toes and minds incarcerated there in White privilege and triviality with a militant beat of the unrequited heat of killed but unkillable memory?

My own argument is that in a strange epiphany of history, this glaring, terrifying, compelling, and hilarious "Something" that has emerged inside the commodified cult of ghettocentricity like a distant flicker of lightning announcing coming storm, is the real truth of the Enlightenment. Kant and company cloistered themselves inside their bourgeois quarters, turned to their own peculiar consciousness and, carefully ignoring all the body parts lower down, found within a universal siren. They imagined the sublime advent of liberty (The "freedom," theorized as a primal noumenal reality for human beings, "sublime" in its ultimate unrepresentability, that is the subject of Kant's second critique) to be a thing without feet or place, untrammeled by desire, unaffected by any requirement save its own irrepressible logic. Here was the universal human subject, realizing its apogee inside Northern European interiority, standing alone, up in the rarified air of pure intentionality, utterly free and master of the entire horizon of bowed and struggling humanity, scattered, pitiably, elsewhere. The image itself was a mirage, but inside the intuition was apparition. There is a universality begging naming inside Enlightenment *hubris* about the planet. The truth is rooted in both time and place.

Conclusion

The universal human carries an African genome and any common outcome to the race's struggle to realize itself in all the diverse materiality of ecology and history must begin with its still throbbing memory of beginnings in a common mother and still probing ancestry that arises like a fountain of irrepressible desire within (Bynum, 1999:73 & 75). The deepest code of that desire is percussive beat, and its contemporary conjuration in hip-hop solicitation poses an ultimate riddle: Can we finally be human together on the surface of a planet that is now made universal and interdependent through the market and technology, in a way that no longer abstracts from genealogy or mobilizes war to try to suppress the root? Or do we perish together in the name of a renegade and impossible desire to reinvent ourselves as mere machinery, the aberrant dream of a scientist in a white robe making the future up without map or memory? Hip-hop is a saving mockery—a surface grotesquery over a base beat felicity that remains an augury. The surface is "black" and confirms the stereotype. The beat is black and beggars the stereotype. The structure is a mobius strip that rips through everyone with a Pan-African soliloquy that still awaits its pedagogy. But even in the absence of such, the glimpse is astonishing. Who could have guessed that a Bronx-Caribbean cultural hybridity, at the turn of the second millennium, would offer a face in the mirror recognizable across the five continents?

5

The African Presence in Caribbean Literature[1]

Mario D. Fenyo

Introduction

En esta tierra, mulata
de africano y español
(Santa Barbara de un lado,
del otro lado, Chango) ...

—Nicolas Guillén, *La Canción del Bongo*

If nothing else, I deserve the reader's praise for being brave (foolhardy, some might say). It did not take me long, after I agreed to examine this aspect of the African connection to realize the impossibility of the undertaking.

As we know, the population of the Caribbean, even in the Dominican Republic or Puerto Rico, suffers from an identity crisis (Dawn Stinchcomb, 2004:1-3), notwithstanding the denials or rejection of that notion. Regardless of the official statistics, the population of the Caribbean islands is overwhelmingly of African ancestry—at least by the United States consensus on what constitutes African lineage. (Perhaps the people of Trinidad and Tobago, and of Guyana, have some justification for rejecting that notion, since those lands are shared by people of African and East Indian ancestry). As regards the gradations of color and the "tax-

---

1. I am indebted, among others, to Dr. Aida Heredia, Dr. Abdul Karim Bangura, Dr. Brenda DoHarris, and Professor Kala Richardson, for feedback and some of the brighter ideas incorporated in this essay. I was also inspired by a seminar held at the University of Missouri in Columbus, in the summer of 2002, under the auspices of Dr. Marvin Lewis and the National Endowment for the Humanities.

onomy" of the inhabitants of the Caribbean islands and surrounding areas, although far from complete, see Vincent Bakpetu Thompson, *The Making of the African Diaspora* (Appendix 2, 1987:411-417).

Indeed, there are a few writers in the Caribbean, whether Anglophone, Francophone, Hispanophone, or even Creole- and Papiamento-speaking, who may be among the exceptions, who may be lacking in African ancestry. That does not negate the fact that the African connection has had an impact on their works as well (e.g., A. Carpentier, V. S. Naipaul, Samuel Selvon, Julia de Burgos, etc.). Since Alexandre Dumas, I know of no writer born in the Caribbean region who has forgotten her or his Caribbean background, or the African presence. While there seems to be relatively little interest in the formal study of "Africana" (see Fierce, passim), Africa is all around us. And if it is not Africa, it is history—the history of slavery, of the slave trade, of colonialism, of racism—all of which curve back to the African continent and its people. As Chinosole writes, "skin as representative of racial consciousness is a metonym for all Afrikans from Egypt and South of the Sahara through the diaspora" (2001:151).

So the question is this: What can be done to circumscribe the topic, to render it more manageable and to enable me to communicate something of value, add to the existing body of knowledge? The following are possible approaches.

(a) One might focus on explicit references to African cultures, to the motherland, to the African continent.

(b) One might attempt to distinguish between the various expressions of Africanism in the different literatures of the region—francophone, hispanophone, anglophone, the many varieties of Creole. As Bangura's meticulous essay in this collection on linguistic connections indicates, there is an almost endless variety of pidginized and Creole languages spoken in the region; these spoken languages become written languages once they become incorporated into a literary work, whether they form the whole work or just a part. Indeed, one might proceed island by island, since the Greater Antilles, and the Lesser ones as well, all have their own body of literature, and one or more Creole languages.

(c) One might reverse the proposition indicated by the title and focus on the impact of the diaspora on African cultures and literature. Obviously, the works of Aimé Césaire, of CLR James, of the Haitian Jacques Roumain, and of so many others have hastened the decolonization of the continent, leading to flag independence, in some cases to real independence. As I noted in an article, the Cameroonian playwright and poet, Elebé Lisembé, based at least one of his plays on Roumain's most famous work, *Gouverneurs de la rosée*, which extols the virtues of collective action, especially when it comes to working the land (in Bangura, 2002:26). Ousmane Sembene, we are told, borrowed items from the same novel in his *O Pays, mon beau peuple* (www.lehman.cuny.edu).

The ideas and actions of Marcus Garvey, of George Padmore, of Eric Williams, of Frantz Fanon were the guides to the struggle for independence in Western, Central and Southern Africa; a second generation of leaders and guiding spirits, including Kwame Touré, Walter Rodney, Fidel Castro, inspired the continued struggle. The Cuban revolution was victorious in 1959. The liberation of Guinea-Bissau, of Zimbabwe, of Angola, of Mozambique, of Namibia ensued, thanks in part to Cuban assistance.

(d) It would also be a worthwhile, major undertaking to try and place Caribbean culture or cultures within the context of the diaspora as a whole. Furthermore, there is the diaspora of the diaspora—the literature produced by Antilians or West Indians who have resettled in London, New York, Paris, and everywhere.

(e) Since I am a student of history by profession, I am tempted to offer a chronological account of the evolution of literatures, taking either the archipelago as a whole, or proceeding language by language, island by island.

(f) Or, one might take the easier way out—as I am doing here—and limit our discussion to a handful of great writers—in other words, my favorites. But where do we start? What would be the logical sequence? Why not start with the grand dame of Caribbean fiction?

Francophony

All of Maryse Condé's fiction has to do with African culture, but there are a few that bear more directly on the African continent, parts of which she knew so well, having lived in Ivory Coast, in Ghana and, of course, in the Guinea of Sekou Touré. She wrote about the glories and struggles of ancient Segou (see *Segu*, 1987 and 1989). She wrote about Guinea in *Heremakhonon* (1976)—the title word meaning "welcome home" in Mande, we are told. The title itself is rather ambivalent, not to say ironic. Indeed, the novel offers a not too flattering portrait of the leader who, albeit unnamed, or referred to simply as Mwalimwana or Leader, bears a strong resemblance to Sekou Touré. That is somewhat disconcerting, if we consider that Touré was viewed by many (including Kwame Touré/Stokely

Carmichael) as one of the most progressive leaders from the period of decolonization, the only one in francophone Africa who stood up to Charles de Gaulle and rejected his neocolonialist solution. In another novel, *Tree of Life*, Condé puts the following words in the mouth of one of her characters: "There are two heads of countries in Africa who are not like those other bastards. The first one, they already got rid of him. That was Kwame Nkrumah. The other is Julius Nyerere ..." (1992:312).

Condé does not mince words: "Africa has been robbed of its grandeur, of its power, of its magnificence." Her polemical analyses are disguised in the form of novels—novels of longing that minimize cultural conflict, in fact, that describe her years in Africa as without "culture clash." In an interview, she explains the difference between her and the people whose skin is white: "I had to go to Africa to discover the meaning and importance of that difference," but the meaning of that difference does not reside in "race" but in "culture" (Interview by Elizabeth Nuñez, www.unesco.org). Time and again the ambivalence of Condé's attitude toward "home," and the African continent in general, comes through. Observing the demeanor of prostitutes in a local bar, she notes that prostitution has been described as the oldest profession, "but, on a closer look, you see that it's just another invention that Africa did not make. Add writing and gunpowder and the list gets longer. These prostitutes bother me. They are proof that Europe has been through these parts" (1992:100). On the other hand, as Condé knows or ought to know, Africans did invent writing.

Francophone writers from earlier generations include the famous René Maran, born in Martinique (Mercer Cook, www.Nathanielturner.com) or on a boat, in transit, according to others (www.ariqueweb.net). He is the author of *Batouala*, of *Le livre de la brousse* [Book of the savanna] and other novels, partly the result of his ten-year stint as a civil servant in what was then the French colony of Equatorial Africa. Although in 1921 *Batouala* was awarded the Prix Goncourt, France's most prestigious literary prize, Maran was nevertheless attacked for adopting the point of view of the African native, denouncing French colonialism in no uncertain terms. In his introduction to *The Wretched of the Earth*, Frantz Fanon wrote, with all the sarcasm he could muster, "as to a revolt, we need not worry at all; what native in his sense would go off to massacre the fair sons of Europe simply to become European as they are? In short, we encouraged these disconsolate spirits and thought it not a bad idea for once to award the Prix Goncourt to a Negro ..." (1963:8-9).

In his preface to *Batouala*, Maran appeals to the writers, "mes Frères de France," asking them to raise their voice against the so-called civilization of the

Europeans, the so-called "mission civilisatrice," the French equivalent of the White Man's Burden. "Civilisation … Tu bâtis ton royaume sur des cadavres" … "La large vie coloniale, si l'on pouvait savoir de quelle quotidienne bassesse elle est faite, on en parlerait moins, on n'en parlerait plus. Elle avilit peu à peu. Rares sont, même parmi les fonctionnaires, les coloniaux qui cultivent leur esprit. Ils n'ont pas la force de resister à l'ambiance. On s'habitue à l'alcool.… Ces excès et d'autres, ignobles, conduisent ceux qui excellent à la veulerie la plus abjecte." It is not too surprising, therefore, that Maran's book was banned in the colonies and Maran himself is eventually forced to resign his post as colonial administrator (www.lehman.cuny.edu).

Indeed, maybe I should have started with the founding father of Negritude, Aimé Césaire. He lived Negritude in his life of action, as mayor of Fort-de-France, the capital of Martinique, and as the Martinican representative in the French General Assembly. He lived Negritude by reclaiming the term "nègre" with its negative connotations, turning it into a badge of honor, and shaping negritude into what Léopold Senghor called "a humanism of the Twentieth century." Negritude, wrote Césaire, is not "a cephalic index, or a plasma, or a soma, but measured by the compass of suffering" (Quoted in Nesbitt, 2002:2). There is no more clear-cut evidence of the intimate connection between the continent and the Caribbean archipelago than the opus of Césaire, as epitomized by his most famous work, *Cahier d'un retour au pays natal.* Although "pays natal" refers to Martinique rather than the African "motherland," the poem did become, according to the Belgian literary historian Lilyan Kesteloot, "the national anthem of blacks the world over" (In Conroy Kennedy, 1975:64):

> Ma négritude n'est pas une pierre, sa surdité ruée contre
> la clameur du jour
> Ma négritude n'est pas une taie d'eau morte sur l'île
> mort de la terre
> ma négritude n'est ni une tour ni une cathédrale
> elle plonge dans la chair rouge du sol
> elle plonge dans la chair ardente du ciel.…

Césaire impressed his readers and critics with his academic and somewhat recondite French, clearly a ploy to gain European recognition for his Antillean or Afro-Antillean cultural heritage. Yet his identification was not exclusively with the "Negro," with the Black person. In the same poem he brings up universals:

Like the hyena-man and the panther-man, he declares, he becomes "un homme-juif/un homme-cafre/un homme-hindou-de-Calcutta/un homme-de-Harlem-qui-ne-vote-pas...." (Quoted in *Toute la Poésie*, 2005:1, www.toutela-poesie.com).

At times, Césaire short-changes negritude, Africa's contributions to civilization. "Nous n'avons inventé ni la poudre, ni la boussole," he asserts in *Cahier d'un retour au pays natal*. Indeed, the Chinese probably deserve credit both for the compass and gunpowder. Yet, in the case of beer, one wonders why Césaire makes the character Lumumba assert, in "A Season in the Congo," that it was one of the good things invented by "white men?" (1956:1).

Hermetic as Césaire's poetry may be, not intended for the simple folk, at other times he was an Afro-Caribbean writing for other Black persons, educated or not. Césaire's plays, all of which are set in an Africentric context, including *La tragédie du roi Cristophe* about the aftermath of the Haitian revolution, *Et les chiens se taisaient,* set in West Africa, and *Une saison au Congo,* about the life and death of Patrice Lumumba, use plain language to convey positive, progressive values. Césaire's best known political statement, however, is his *Discourse on Colonialism,* speaking out against colonialism and, by implication, against neocolonialism, in plain yet eloquent terms. It is perhaps ironic that the two most determined and eloquent antagonists of colonialism, Césaire and Frantz Fanon, both hail from the French West Indies which have moved, since World War II, further away from independence than ever, to become an "integral" part of "metropolitan" France.

Jacques Roumain in Haiti wrote the best-known Haitian novel (I hope Edwidge Danticat will forgive me), *Gouverneurs de la rosée,* which was translated into many languages ["Masters of the Dew" in English] and achieved international fame, partly because of the author's Communist connections. (He was the founder of the Communist Party of Haiti) (See Léon François Hofmann "Présentation de Gouverneurs de la Rosée [sic]"). The collective is central to Roumain's world view, much as the village is central to George Lamming's *In the Castle of my Skin*, where the characters are frequently described by their function in the Village, spelled with an upper-case V. Indeed, in the Barbadian context, "the Village sings, the Village dances" (Chinosole, 2001:74-75). For Roumain as well as for Lamming, a meaningful, productive existence can be achieved more easily within the community, as part of the community, as part of a collective existence.

Roumain, we are told, was a light-complexioned mulatto—in Haiti, where such things matter. While he had traveled across Europe, apparently he had never reached the African continent. He had good information, however; he was inspired by the Haitian anthropologist, J. Price Mars, who described the cultural riches of African civilizations, and identified the African cultural transferences to Haiti (Conroy Kennedy, 1975:17). Like DuBois, Roumain became a bourgeois turncoat but, unlike DuBois, he rejected his European forefathers, a mere "spit" upon these shores, to become a Black revolutionary. In his collection of poems, *Bois d'ébène*, dating from 1939, he wrote that "Negro peddler or revolt/you know all the roadways of the world since you were sold in Guinea ..." (Conroy Kennedy, 1975: 23). Further on, he writes that "Africa I have kept your memory, Africa you are within me ..." (Conroy Kennedy, 1975:25).

One indication of the vastness of the topic we are confronting is the monograph by Andre Ntonfo, a Cameroonian scholar. The monograph, some 210 pages long, entitled *Le roman indigéniste haitien: esthétique et idéologie* (1997), discusses the works of Roumain along with those of 11 other "indigenist" writers from Haiti. Thus, it is clear that this chapter on the literary connections between Africa and the Caribbean can do little more than skim the surface.

Others in the Caribbean are in search of a Creole identity, participating in a cultural independence movement, extolling hybridization, nevertheless recognizing and paying homage to the African roots. An example of this tendency is the work of Patrick Chamoiseau (Chanda, www.france.diplomatic.fr). Everywhere in the region, the younger generation tends to demonstrate its consciousness of a culture that not only transcends geography and language, but searches for the "routes" (rather than the "roots"), the commerce between cultures which, however complex, is more apt to explain the hybridization—using that term in its most positive sense—that takes place in the Caribbean region (Jay, 1999:176-194).

Hispanophony

Instead of the francophone or franco-Creole body of literature, one might start with Cuba, the island-nation which, in spite of ongoing attempts to isolate it, has engaged in such "extraordinary activity" as a "promoter, critic, and publisher of things Latin American ..." writes Robert Marquez (1974:31). Nicolas Guillén, who ranks alongside Pablo Neruda or César Vallejo as the great Latin American poet and progressive intellect of the 20th Century, did not reject or disguise his African ancestry. To the contrary, he assumes that practically all Cubans are of mixed blood (i.e. Black, by United States standards), and decided it should be a source of pride. "The spirit of Cuba is mestizo," he writes. "All of us are somewhat black" (Angel Augier's introduction to Nicolas Guillén, *Obra Poética*, 1974:xxviii). "The African inoculation in this land is so deep, and cross and intersect in our network of social waterways with so many capillary currents, that it would demand the work of a miniaturist to unknot the hieroglyph" (Guillen's own introduction to the volume of poetry *Songoro Cosongo*, 1974:114). He integrated music into his poems, the music of the *son*, which like practically all music one hears in the Caribbean, owes ultimately to Africa:

> Yambambo, yambambé!
> Repica el congo solongo,
> Repica el Negro bien Negro;
> Congo solongo del Songo
> Baila yambo sobre un pié.
>
> Mamatomba,
> serembe cuseremba.
>
> El Negro canta y se ajuma,
> el Negro se ajuma y canta
> el Negro canta y se va.
>
> Ac“ememe serembó,
> ae;
>   yambó,
>   ae.
>
> Tamba, tamba, tamba, tamba
> tambe del negro que tumba;
> tumba del Negro, caramba,
> caramba, que el negro tumba:
> Yamba, yambo, yambambé!

Or, in his *Son Número 6* from another collection of poems:

> Yoruba soy, lloro en Yoruba
> Lucumí.
> Como soy un yoruba de Cuba,
> quiero hasta Cuba suba mi llanto Yoruba

que suba el alegre llanto Yoruba
que sale de mi.

Yoruba soy,

Cantando voy,

Llorando estoy,

Y cuando no soy Yoruba,

Soy congo, mandinga, carabalí.…

Of course, I could devote the rest of this chapter to reading or reciting verses by Guillen, but that would hardly be fair to Nancy Morejón and dozens of others. Guillén's disciple, and the most famous poet of Cuba today, Nancy Morejón, also asserts the "Afro-Cuban essence" (1979:3). Her best-known poem, *Mujer negra*, is an epic of the African woman from the Middle Passage, through enslavement, through self-emancipation and maroonage, to the Cuban revolution—in which the poet speaks in the first person singular, assuming the identity of all those women through the ages (Phaf, 1999:539). Although her hosts during her infrequent visits to the United States have attempted to portray her as a closet foe of the Cuban revolution who has no choice but to keep her feelings to herself or disguise them altogether, she has been and continues to be part of that revolution, especially its attempt to fully integrate and enhance the culture of the overwhelmingly Black (or mulatto) population of the island.

In addition to her Africentricity, Morejón has been described as a "womanist" (Davies, 1997), which is the term often used for "colored" women who fight for their rights, while rejecting the label "feminist" because of its white and bourgeois implications. Womanists, as we know, are women-activists from the Caribbean, the African continent and other areas of the Third World.

Luis Pales Matos is the Puerto Rican exponent of Africanism—also known as Afro-Antillean poetry, *afroantillanismo*, *Negrismo* (rather different from the Negritude of Césaire and Senghor), or *poesía negra*. Many of his poems in the collection "Tuntún de pasa y griferia" consciously reject the canons of Hispanic and Western literature, to adopt African rhythms, African sounds, or sounds and rhythms he imagines are akin to the African (Branche, 1999:494). According to one of the positive critics, the poetry of Pales Matos is an idealization of the African body, of the African sounds, of the past and present in Puerto Rico (Rivera Casellas, 1999:635). Unlike Guillén, Pales Matos is generally described as a "White" poet, and the paradox—looking at *negrismo* from the "outside," as opposed to "from the inside" in the case of Guillen—has been noted by a number of critics. As the critic Julio Marzan observed, "leftist poets rejected Pales Matos as a racist who ridiculed and exploited African culture." For instance, in Pales Matos' poetry, the Haitian aristocracy after liberation mimics the French aristocracy, and this is described in simian terms, sometimes even as savages and cannibals; their representatives include the "Duque de la Mermelada" or "Madama de Cafolé" (Branche, 1999:489). The islands of Martinique and Guadeloupe are described in feminine terms—at a time when women were the ones expected to do the house-chores—the former as the one who cooks the soup while the latter makes the bed. The loving provided by the "mulata" is described in stereotypical terms as "amor sin trabas y sin prisas" (Branche, 1999:491).

In contrast, Guillén, a true Black voice (or mulatto, if you prefer) and a Marxist, appeared to speak more directly to the condition of the Third World. The trouble with this analysis, however, is that it pits Pales against Guillén, whereas Pales preceded, and perhaps inspired, Guillén. Pales was well aware of the distorted reality of Puerto Rico, the tension between the romanticized official culture of the island—the mountain, the *criollo*, the *jíbaro*—and the coastal plain, with its reality of African blood. It is possible to view his effort as one to vindicate the language of the people, the real Puerto Rican, a language of sounds with which everyone could understand and identify (Marzan, 1995:506-523).

Julia de Burgos, the outstanding woman-poet of Puerto Rico or, more simply, the outstanding poet of Puerto Rico—who would have deserved the Nobel prize along with Chilean Gabriela Mistral—also indulged in Negrismo, in at least one of her poem. Furthermore, the river Loiza, which flows through the most authentically African settlements on the island becomes, in her poem, titled *Rio Grande de Loiza,* a quintessentially Puerto Rican river: "Muy señor rio mio. Rio hombre. Unico hombre/que ha besado mi alma al besar en mi cuerpo." In *Ay ay ay de la grifa negra*, she identifies herself as pure Negro or, to be more exact, she pretends to be Black, the grand-daughter of a slave. A feminist before that ideology was anything but fashionable, and a nationalist when nationalism was a crime in Puerto Rico (it still is), her motives in giving Black people a voice in her poetry are above suspicion. Nationalism, in the Puerto Rican context, meant freedom from control by the United States, and independence from the United States in those days meant primarily the rejection of racism, ideals personified by Albizu Campos, the leader of the Nationalist Party, and himself a Black man.

While in New York, where de Burgos died in the streets of Harlem, the victim of alcoholism, and where she lived part of her life, she became an advocate of Black civil rights. "In the 1930s," according to her anonymous biographer, "she joined other Caribbean writers in a literary protest against European colonialism and its denigration of African culture. Negritude, as the movement was called, promoted the idea that artists of African descent must look to their African heritage for inspiration rather than rely on Western traditions and aesthetics." (www.gale.com).

Another Puerto Rican voice that should not be overlooked is that of Jose Celso Barbosa who struggled throughout much of his life, pro and con, against and on the side of pride in his African ancestry. At one point, he embraced it with enthusiasm, proclaiming "Negro! Negro! Negro!/Y bien! Estamos orgullosos de serlo ..." (Labrador-Rodriguez, 1999:722).

If I am to bring the analysis up-to-date, I would have to mention a younger generation of poets responding to the African heritage—Blas Jimenez foremost among them. The context of his work is the Dominican Republic which resembles Puerto Rico in the sense that it has yet to come to terms with its "Africano en despertar"—the awakening of its African consciousness. He confronts the repression of "Blackness by exposing Caribbean and Dominican racism through his poetry" (Tillis, 2003:29-38). "Caribe/muere tu juventud/por ideales revolucionarias/en tradiciones importadas ..." Unlike the politically more progressive Dominican poet Pedro Mir, he rejects not only the gringo or American influences, but also the Cuban and the Russian, for their "revolution is televised" [*La nueva revolución*], finding only Eric Williams, the historian and founding father of Trinidad and Tobago, worthy of praise (Tillis, 2003:7). Much like Edwidge Danticat in *The Farming of Bones*, he evokes and deplores the murder of thousands of Haitian migrant workers—Trujillo's effort to "whiten" his country. (Tillis, 2003:7)

Anglophony

Anglophone Caribbean literature includes two Nobel-prize winners (Naipaul and Derek Walcott), and a wide range of noteworthy literary and political accomplishments. V. S. Naipaul and Samuel Selvon have written some of the most enjoyable and most humorous stories ever (see *Miguel Street* by Naipaul, or *Ways of Sunlight* by Selvon), using various varieties of Trinidadian Creole, indirectly African-inspired—indirectly, for the authors happen to be of East Indian ancestry, and the protagonists of their stories are barely educated workers and members of the "under-class" who have little awareness of their own ethnic and cultural background. The African connection lies precisely in the fact that their cultural identity has been taken away from them; while they have preserved their humanity to a large extent, there is nothing particularly African about it. They are often comic figures, or figures of derision, characters for the reader, including the white and European reader, at whom to laugh. In his travelogue, *The Middle Passage*, Naipaul is not concerned with the slave trade directly, but rather with the interaction between ethnic groups on those islands of the archipelago and in the surrounding lands (Guyana, Suriname) Afro-Caribbeans share harmoniously, or in discord, with the descendants of Indian "coolies."

For the other recipient of the Nobel Prize in literature, Derek Walcott, "hybridization" is not a source of pride, rather it is a source of self-conscious struggle (Bradley, www.postcolonialweb.org). In his poem, *A Far Cry from Africa*, he confronts his own divided loyalties between Africa and Britain. The British are not spared his contempt: they are, or at least were, "the worm, colonial of carrion ..." Can he choose "between this Africa and the English tongue I love?" And the concluding line asks: "How can I turn from Africa and live?" Of course, such questions are academic. The admission and recognition of African ancestry is what counts; it becomes a point of honor not to reject it.

This erudite and thoroughly Westernized poet confronts his African heritage on a number of occasions. As had C.L.R. James, Eugene O'Neill, and others before him, as a playwright, he also tackled the contradictions in the acts and character of the Haitian Emperor Henri Christophe.

The novels of the Trinidadian Earl Lovelace belong in a different category. In his case, we have the work of an author of African ancestry; although a sense of humor permeates his work also, the humor is often self-directed. His characters have not severed their relations to Africa; they are consciously African with their background of enslavement—even though slavery in Trinidad lasted little more than a generation (as opposed to Tobago and most other Caribbean islands, where it lasted for centuries). "Guinea John," writes Lovelace at the beginning of *Salt*, "with his black jacket on and a price of two hundred pounds sterling on his head, made his way to the East Coast [of Trinidad], mounted the cliff at Manzanilla, put two corn cobs under his armpits and flew away to Africa, taking with him the mysteries of levitation and flight, leaving the rest of his family still in captivity mourning over his selfishness, everybody putting in their mouth and saying 'You see! You see! That is why Black people children doomed to suffer: their own parents refuse to pass on the knowledge that they know to them.'" (Lovelace, 1998:3).

During the inebriation and optimism accompanying decolonization, explains Lovelace, the politicians "chanted the mantras" that would liberate them: the list includes Socrates, Tacitus, Timbuktu, Tagore, Delhi, Nkrumah, Nehru, Gandhi, Senghor, Toussaint, Césaire ..." A Greek, a Roman, four East Indian, and five African names ..." (1998:35). Lovelace writes of "Orisha priests and Bush doctor" ancestors in Trinidad, and people getting arrested for the practice of Obeah ... (1998:23, 89). His characters have to choose between their own cultural heritage and the prosperity promised by assimilation and modernization. The protagonist of *Salt*, a teacher at one point in his life, reads and discusses *anancy* stories in class. At one point, he explains: "Here am I, more African than any African and no place in Africa to go to. I don't know which part I come from ... He had no idea of the sky in that place, of the land, of the roads, of the shape of the leaves, of the smell of the earth, of his people in the setting of that home. He had no idea of their dances, of their songs, of the language. He had no idea of the loss he had lost ..." (Lovelace, 1998:173).

As Lovelace writes, "progress in a community is not measured by what Government provides but chiefly by what the community is prepared to do for itself to resolve its own problems" (Quoted in www.bookrags.com) Lovelace's ideas become widely disseminated, not only because of his expanding base of readers, but also because *Salt* was awarded the Commonwealth Writers' Prize. Thus, radical and iconoclastic ideas are sometimes rewarded by the establishment, acting against its own interests or exercising a great deal of foresight.

It would be unfair to by-pass Jamaica, with its rich body of poetry, of reggae, of indigenous fiction. The Rastafarians, whether described as religion or movement, owe their very existence to the African connection, pay almost exclusive homage to Africa, as summed up in the person of the ruler of Ethiopia. This relationship takes the form of music and literature in the work of some of the classics of reggae.

The Jamaican Claude McKay, for one, has earned international fame, because of his participation in the Harlem Renaissance. He has even been described as the "true inventor of Negritude" by no less of an authority than Léopold Senghor (Nesbitt, 2002:2). His *Banana Bottom* has been used as required reading in some school districts in the United States. Bita, the protagonist of the novel, sponsored by a White missionary couple, attended school in England, but returns to the island and gradually finds her roots. Her roots are in the Jamaican village, Banana Bottom, where we also encounter Obeah religion and West African vocabulary such as the term b*eke,* used among the natives to refer to a "white person," transplanted directly from Nigeria (as are the terms *oyibo, oyinbo, bature,* etc.). At one point in the novel, there is a discussion of African art. The objects discussed had been brought from Africa by another missionary couple, and are described as "idols" and as "grotesque," a "show and tell" lesson designed to demonstrate that the "African cousins still lived in savagery." Bita, however, realizes, along with the author McKay, that these objects are indeed works of art, originating from some genuine system of belief and presenting an African "vision of life" (McKay, 2005:197-198). Africa, however, writes Paul Jay, adopting the model introduced by Paul Gilroy in his *The Black Atlantic*, is not so much the "roots," as part of the "routes," a component of a complex "commerce" of cultures. The term hybridization is used in its most positive sense (Jay, 1999:182-183).

In a balkanized archipelago such as the Caribbean, political considerations are almost never absent; all the more so in a culture or cultures where "race" is a dominant feature. This is true even in the case of authors who do not insist on centering their analysis on Blackness or Black Power, such as C.L.R. James. Writing about Frank Worrell, the first Black captain of the West Indian cricket team, he "cannot see that Barbadian as an exemplar of Blackness." About a Black baseball player, he asks the academic question: "Does Sobers bat, bowl and field black?" (Quoted in King, 2001:4). Having become acquainted with the works of Marx, C.L.R James joined a Trotskyist movement, only to split from that group and, like Césaire, appalled by the Soviet repression of the Hungarian Revolution of 1956 (see Henry and Buhle, 1992:passim), formed his own splinter group. His meeting with Leon Trotsky in Mexico only confirmed his perception that race is, after all, a primary socio-political factor. Yet he was deported from the United States in 1953, not because of race, but his radical politics. He spent time with Kwame Nkrumah in Ghana, not because of race but, like W.E.B. DuBois, because of the progressive views they shared.

For C.L.R. James, the interaction between Africa and the West Indies was more a current of ideas flowing *from* the Caribbean. "The recognition of Africanism, the agitation for the recognition of Africa, the literary creation of an African ideology, all were directly the creation of West Indians (Garvey, Padmore, Césaire, among others)" he writes (quoted in Henry and Buhle, 1992:181). He adds, however, that these West Indians were interpreting Western thought, presumably for the sake of enhancing Pan-Africanism.

If we accept Edouard Glissant's aphorism, that History and Literature form part of the same problematic, we must also accept the notion that James's *Black Jacobins* is not only a great history book, but a literary masterpiece as well. Of course, there is no need to stretch an argument to demonstrate that James was a literary figure, for that is self-evident, even if we disregard his well-known novel, *Minty Alley* or his play *Toussaint L'Ouverture*, which centers on the function of Vodun. Vodun or Vodoo, of course, is both an African religion and a syncretic religion based in Haiti. In *Jacobins*, James writes: "I was tired of reading and hearing about Africans being persecuted and oppressed in Africa, in the Middle Passage, in the USA and all over the Caribbean. I made up my mind that I would write a book in which Africans or people of African descent instead of being constantly the object of other people's exploitation and ferocity would themselves be taking action on a grand scale and shaping other people to their own needs" (quoted in King, 2001:31). Nevertheless, James remains true to his political self. That his political self was Marxist, socialist and progressive, goes without saying. It also goes for practically all outstanding Caribbean intellectuals who chose to write.

Conclusion

What are the lessons to be learnt? It makes little sense to discuss post-modern and post-colonial reality in literature without reference to the political and the social. Apart from the obvious fact that the Caribbean was the major beneficiary of the African diaspora, where even the "whitest" island-nations are largely Black and wholly mixed (or "hybrid" to use the fashionable jargon), there is an obvious set of facts to stress: the islands of the Caribbean—whether Anglophone, hispanophone or francophone—do have a literature in common, inspired and perhaps determined by the African presence; indeed, they have a culture in common, from Trinidad and Guyana in the South, to Cuba and beyond in the North and the West. And if they have common elements in literature—not to mention music, cuisines, and so much else, the long-awaited pan-Caribbean federation no longer seems merely utopian or just the crazy dream of some West Indian patriot. In addition to climate and geography, economics, common history, commlon cuisines, etc., the diaspora, the African element, is what provides the archipelago with its cultural harmony.

The new federation is just beyond the horizon!

6

African Origins of and Influences on the Diasporic Population: Evidence from the Linguistic Presuppositions of the African, Jamaican, and Negro National Anthems

Abdul Karim Bangura

Introduction

One out of every five Africans lives outside the African continent. The great majority of these Africans are in the Western Hemisphere. Some are now native speakers of Spanish, like the African Cubans. Some have grown up with the Portuguese tongue, like the African Brazilians. Still others are part of the French-speaking world, scattered from Haiti to Martinique. There are also a few Arabic-speakers throughout the Middle East. But the largest single group outside the African continent comprises African Saxons: that is, African Americans, African Jamaicans, African Trinidadians, African Britons, and African Canadians (Mazrui 1977:68).

The slave trade was the most significant catalyst in dispersing Africans to other parts of the world. But it was not until late in the 19th Century and in the course of the 20th Century that Pan-Africanism as a movement of African solidarity got under way (Mazrui 1977:68), leading to a significant number of investigations about linguistic, social, and cultural connections between Africa and its Diaspora.

The debate over the linguistic, social, and cultural connections between Africa and its Diaspora, however, has been controversial since Melville J. Herskovits' pioneering work was published in 1941. The debate was heightened when E. Franklin Frazier's work was published in 1963. While Herskovits proposed that African linguistic, social, and cultural features have survived in North America and have been retained by a process of acculturation and adaptation, Frazier emphasized African linguistic, social, and cultural discontinuity and advocated a deculturalization hypothesis.

What all these works demonstrate is that the almost total absence of visible African artifacts in African Diaspora culture does not warrant the view that nothing African survived the tyranny of slavery. While the visible artifacts of religious sculpture gradually disappeared, subtler linguistic and communicative artifacts were sustained and embellished by the Africans' creativity. What this chapter does is survey some of these complex linguistic connections, which constitute continuity and relationship between Africa and its Diaspora.

Toward this end, this chapter presents a textual analysis of three African Diasporic anthems: the African National Anthem, *Nkosi Sikelel'i Afrika*; the Jamaican National Anthem, *Jamaica*; and the Negro National Anthem, *Lift Ev'ry Voice and Sing*. By analyzing the texts of these anthems using presuppositions,[1] within a linguistic framework,[2] it is suggested that previous studies which have examined national anthems and other textual political symbols[3] in terms of their valuable functions in the lives of political systems are quite limited for understanding their meanings. An examination of the texts of the three anthems clearly shows that national anthems, like other textual political symbols, convey not only surface contents, but a great deal of auxiliary contents as well. The major thesis in this chapter, then, is the following: Analyses of national anthems or other textual political symbols that fail to account for linguistic presuppositions risk ignoring relevant contents that may be central to the texts' meanings.

Consequently, this chapter is also about the possibility that significant *functional* explanations of textual political symbols can be evaluated using linguistic features. The essence of an approach of this nature is captured by Levinson when he suggests:

> Most recent linguistic explanations have tended to be internal to linguistic theory: that is to say, some linguistic feature is explained by reference to other linguistic features, or to aspects of the theory itself. But there is another possible kind of explanation, often more powerful, in which some linguistic feature is motivated by principles outside the scope of linguistic theory (1983:40).

Available analyses of textual political symbols have been conducted by political analysts. But because these political analysts lack the necessary tools for delineating the linguistic structures inherent in these textual political symbols, their analyses have been limited to functional explanations.

By employing a presuppositional approach to analyze the texts of the three national anthems, the ideas underlying these political symbols can be illuminated. This is possible because in the study of linguistic texts, as in the study of physics, special instruments, formulae, and laboratories beyond the grasp of the uninitiated can be utilized. Because one trained in linguistics possesses analytical skills and tools, and concepts that permit insights into the nature of language in general, s/he is in a better position than a political analyst to explain the formal linguistic structures which constitute cues as to how the writers intended their textual political symbols to be interpreted.

Thus, the major question in this chapter is the following: What salient linguistic presuppositions are embedded in the texts of the three national anthems and how can they be explained? In exploring this question, the systematic application of discovery procedures well-known in linguistic pragmatics will help to uncover propositions that will illuminate the texts for current readers.

In order to accomplish the preceding objectives, the rest of this chapter is divided into five interrelated major sections: (1) Synopsis of Previous Studies on Political Symbols, (2) Methodology, (3) Contexts of the Discourses of the Three National Anthems, (4) Analysis, and (5) Conclusion. The originality of this chapter consists, therefore, in the clarity with which familiar but unconnected facts about the texts of the three national anthems are marshaled into a simpler, linguistically satisfying unity.

Synopsis of Previous Studies on Political Symbols

Previous studies on political symbols have examined such symbols in terms of their valuable functions in the lives of political systems. They are said to be important in promoting social integration, fostering legitimacy, inducing loyalty, gaining compliance, and providing citizens with security and hope (Edelman 1964, Jones 1964, Lasswell 1965, Merelman 1966, Cobb and Elder 1976 1983).

Because these studies have done very little empirical research on what political symbols, more specifically, the American Constitution, mean to the public, Bass (1979) takes the first step towards examining the symbolic meaning of the American Constitution and its development. Using Q sort, correlation, and factor analysis statistical techniques, Baas finds that the Constitution is a vague, diffuse and distant symbol which is given specific meaning in terms of concrete primary figures and/or images.

While all of these studies are quite useful for understanding political symbols, they nevertheless tell us nothing about the auxiliary contents of these symbols, especially the textual ones. The relevant contents that may be central to the meanings of these symbols therefore need to be explored. The question that emerges here, then, is the following: How can this be done?

Methodology

As stated in the introductory section of this chapter, the method employed here to analyze the texts of the three national anthems is *linguistic presuppositional analysis*. This approach is based on the premise that there exist in every discourse some background assumptions against which the main import of utterances or statements can be assessed (Levinson 1983:173).

The rhetorical tactic of presupposition in political discourse is by now familiar to many linguists. A paradigm example is the opponent's query, "Has the President stopped siphoning the country's funds to his Swiss bank account?" Without explicitly making the assertion, the opponent implicates that the President has indeed been siphoning the country's funds to his (the President's) Swiss bank account. Less contentious presuppositions can be suggested as well: that the President is a male, and that the President has a Swiss bank account. This example illustrates the fact that speakers or writers often express more than they assert. Their utterances or scripts convey not only their surface contents, but a great deal of auxiliary content as well.

In the data analysis section, the linguistic presuppositions extracted from the texts of the three national anthems are identified and analyzed. In the remainder of this section, the concept (presupposition) is defined and its scope clearly delimited. This is done by briefly examining the concept as it has developed in the philosophical and linguistic literature.[4]

Logical Presupposition

The phenomenon of linguistic presupposition can be traced back to the philosophical writings of Gottlob Frege (1892/1952). He raised many of the issues that later became central to the discussion of presupposition. According to Frege, "If anything is asserted there is always an obvious presupposition (*voraussetzung*) that the simple or compound proper names used have a reference" (1952:69).

A later exchange between Bertrand Russell (1905, 1957) and Peter Strawson (1950, 1952) brought the notion of presupposition more fully into scholarly discourse. Russell, in his first essay on the subject (1905), argued that Frege's views were simply wrong. Struggling with the problem of how to account for the fact that sentences lacked proper referents, Russell came up with conclusions that were different from those of Frege.

Russell's analysis remained unchallenged until Strawson, in his 1950 essay, suggested a different approach. For Strawson, many of the puzzles in Russell's essay emerged from a failure to distinguish sentences from uses of sentences to make, for instance, statements that are true or false. Consider the following sentences:

(1) The President of Ethiopia is a tyrant.

(2) The President of Ethiopia is not a tyrant.

(3) There is one and only one President of Ethiopia.

In his analysis of definite descriptions, Russell suggested that propositions of the form (1) entail presuppositions of the form (3). Strawson did not agree with this suggestion. Instead, Strawson pointed out that (2), the negation of (1), does not affect the truth conditions of (3). If the relation between (1) and (3) were one of entailment, then, by *modus ponens*[5] (2) could not entail (3). One's linguistic intuitions tell him/her, however, that if *either* (1) or (2) is true, then, (3) is also true. Strawson labeled the relation one of presupposition, which he formally designated as:

(4) Sentence S_1 logically presupposes sentence S_2 iff the truth of S_2 is a precondition for the truth or falsity of S_1 (1952:175).

The practical approach for distinguishing presuppositions from entailments is the employment of the traditional *constancy under negation* rule. One sentence is said to presuppose another if and only if the sentence and its negation both require it to be true.

Semantic Presupposition and Implications for Logic

Intrigued by Strawson's account of presupposition, formal linguists sought to build semantic theory upon the foundational relation of semantic entailment defined in (5), and had hoped to advance a more convincingly logical account of natural language by suggesting the relation of semantic presupposition defined in (6), as follows:

(5) S_1 semantically entails S_2 (written S_1, ⊩S), iff every situation that makes S_1 true makes S_2 true.

(6) A sentence S_1 semantically presupposes a sentence S_2 iff S_1 ⊩S and $\sim S_1$ ⊩S_2.

In order to incorporate the relation of semantic presupposition into a formal natural-language semantics, a logical framework that is different from the standard calculi is called for. This means that *bivalence*[6] and *modus tollens*[7] must be given up in order to meet the requirement for semantic presupposition. If a sentence S_1 semantically presupposes a sentence S_2, then, by definition (6), S_1 entails S_2 and $\sim S_1$ entails S_2. *Modus tollens* must thus be given up. For without *bivalency*, in propositions of the form p6q, the falsity of the consequent could not falsify the condition. The consequent might instead result in the truth value 'neither true nor false.'

Presuppositional Defeasibility

Presuppositional defeasibility refers to the fact that presuppositions are liable to evaporate in certain contexts, either immediate linguistic contexts, less immediate discourse contexts, or in cases where contrary assumptions are made. The defeasibility of presuppositions in particular discourse contexts, for example, can defeat any context-free semantic account as illustrated below:

(7) Kwame N'Krumah was overthrown from the presidency before he could realize his dream of a united Africa.

(8) Kwame N'Krumah realized his dream of a united Africa.

(9) Kwame N'Krumah died before he could realize his dream of a united Africa.

The connectives 'before' and 'after' ordinarily trigger the presuppositions of their complements, as (7) presupposes (8). But in (9), the meaning of 'before' (temporal priority) plus background knowledge about death defeat the presupposition of (8). Individuals ordinarily do not realize their dreams after their deaths.

In this situation, temporal logic will not help. Presuppositions are defeasible within many constructions such as those in the following sentences.

(10) If Thabo Mbeki invites Lansana Conte to South Africa, he will regret having a murderer as his guest.

(11) If Thabo Mbeki invites Abdoulaye Wade to South Africa, he will regret having a murderer as his guest.

(12) Thabo Mbeki will have a murderer as his guest.

The sentence (11) presupposes (12), but (10) does not. Since Lansana Conte is well known for his murderous campaigns in Guinea whose invitation Thabo Mbeki will regret, the conditional clause in (10) defeats the presupposition of (12). The fact that Abdoulaye Wade is not generally thought to be a murderer, 'murderer' in (11) must refer to someone else and the conditional clause does not defeat the presupposition.

Examples such as this would place presupposition outside the domain of context-free logical semantics, but within the scope of a context-sensitive linguistic semantics. The incorporation of propositions drawn from lexical entries, nonetheless, fails to account for all forms of presuppositional defeasibility. The contents of the following discourse, for example, can defeat a presupposition:

(13) We need to find out which African leaders are on the payroll of the United States Central Intelligence Agency (CIA). John Stockwell would certainly know. I have discussed the issue with him. John Stockwell is not aware that Mobutu is on the payroll of the CIA. So John Stockwell can be trusted.

The sentence 'John Stockwell is not aware that Mobutu is on the payroll of the CIA' would ordinarily presuppose that 'Mobutu is on the payroll of the CIA.' But the preceding discourse defeats this presupposition. It appears that any semantics of presupposition, then, calls for access to the discourse context in order to detect defeated presuppositions. As in the case of lexical access, the mechanisms needed to account for presuppositions gravitate away from semantics and toward pragmatics in this case as well.

Iterative presuppositional defeat causes more havoc. Consider this example.

(14) It isn't Buthelezi who will become our next head of state.

(15) Someone will become our next head of state.

Ordinarily, sentence (14) will presuppose sentence (15). Suppose, however, that each potential head of state in South Africa had asked the utterer of (14), 'Will I be the next head of state?' to which the response is 'No.' By iterating over the set of potential heads of state and proposing that each, in turn, will not be the next head of state, the presupposition in (15) is defeated. Appeals to lexical knowledge will definitely fail to explain the defeat of the presupposition in this example. Reference to the *deictic context*[8] of the discourse is necessary in order to explain the defeat of the presupposition of (15).

The Projection Problem

There exist two sides to the projection problem. The first is that presuppositions tend to survive in linguistic contexts where entailments cannot. More precisely, the presuppositions of component sentences are inherited by the whole complex sentence where the entailments of those components would not be. The second is that presuppositions tend to disappear in other contexts where one might expect them to survive, and where entailments would.

Beginning with the kind of context in which presuppositions survive where entailments do not, the examples that follow suggest that one may, but need not, take this as a defining characteristic of presuppositions.

(16) The President appointed five military officers.

(17) There is a President.

(18) The President appointed three military officers.

If sentence (16) is negated, as in (19), the entailment (18) does not survive, but the presupposition (17) does; this being of course the initial observation from which presuppositional theories emerged.

(19) The President did not appoint five military officers.

In a similar manner, presuppositions survive in other kinds of contexts in which entailments do not. An example is modal contexts: that is, those embedding under modal operators such as *possible, may be, most probably*, etc. Consequently, (20) continues to presuppose (17).

(20) It is possible that the President appointed five military officers.

It is obvious, however, that (20) does not entail (18). One cannot logically infer from the mere possibility of a state of affairs that any part of it is actual.

Presuppositions tend to distinguish themselves by their ability to survive in different sets of contexts like compound sentences formed by connectives *and, or, if … then* and their equivalents. Consider the following examples:

(21) The two chief's sons are hired again this term, which entails *inter alia,* (22) and presupposes (23) because of the iterative *again.*

(22) A chief's son is hired this term.

(23) The two chief's sons had been hired before.

If (21) is embedded in the antecedent of a conditional like in (24),

(24) If the two chief's sons are hired again this term, Olusegun Obasanjo will get the support he desperately needs,

it is evident that (22) is not an entailment of (24), but the presupposition (23) survives.

Now turning to the second aspect of the projection problem, in which presuppositions of lower clauses sometimes fail to be inherited by the whole complex sentence, one would observe that presuppositions are sometimes defeasible because of *intra-sentential* context.

Presuppositions can be overtly *denied* in co-ordinate sentences such as these:

(25) Chinua Achebe didn't manage to become President.

(26) Chinua Achebe tried to become President.

(27) Chinua Achebe didn't manage to become President; he didn't even run.

Here, (25) presupposes (26), but overt denial defeats it in (27).

In addition, to the overt denial of presuppositions, they can also be suspended in conditional clauses, as for example in the following:

(28) Daniel arap Moi didn't lie to the Kenyan people again about leaving office.

(29) Daniel arap Moi previously lied to the Kenyan people about leaving office.

(30) Danieal arap Moi didn't lie to the Kenyan people again about leaving office; if indeed he ever did.

In this example, (28) presupposes (29), but the condition in (30) defeats it.

In sum, the preceding discussion clearly suggests that semantic theories of presupposition are not viable. This is mainly because semantics is more concerned with the specification of invariant, stable meanings that can be associated with expressions.

Pragmatic Presupposition

Because presuppositions are not invariant and they are not stable, they became an ideal unit of linguistic analysis for pragmaticists. Earlier pragmatic theories of presupposition offered little more than possible definitions for the concept using pragmatic notions (Gazdar 1979:103ff offers a list of these definitions and a discussion). Despite their differing terminology, these definitions have been subsumed by Levinson (1983: 204-205) into two basic concepts: (a) *appropriateness* (or *felicity*), and (b) *mutual knowledge* (or *common ground*, or *joint assumption*) indicated as follows:

(31) An utterance A *pragmatically presupposes* a proposition B iff A is *appropriate* only if B is *mutually known* by participants.

Levinson, however, argues that the utility of the notion of appropriateness is objectionable and that the mutual knowledge condition is far too strong. He supports Gazdar's (1979:105) suggestion that what one presupposes is *consistent with* the propositions assumed in the context (Levinson 1983:205).

Consequently, an earlier definition of pragmatic presupposition by Stalnaker (1974) is still prevalent today. He defines this concept in the following way:

(32) A proposition **P** is a pragmatic presupposition of a speaker just in case the speaker assumes or believes that **P**, assumes or believes that his addressee assumes or believes that **P**, and assumes or believes that his addressee recognized that he is making these assumptions (Stalnaker 1974:200).

Stalnaker's definition suggests that, unless they explicitly object, participants in a discourse implicitly accept the presuppositions of the utterances of other participants. Consequently, the addressee's failure to object to infelicitous presuppositions would violate Grice's maxim of quantity, which calls for a participant's contribution to a discourse be as informative as required for the purpose of communication (for more on this maxim, refer to Grice 1957).

In a later study, Stalnaker (1978) discerns two types of discourse contexts: *defective* and *non-defective*. The former contexts, according to Stalnaker, are inherently unstable and necessarily result in efforts to equilibrate the "context sets" of participants. The latter contexts, Stalnaker suggests, are the "context sets," or the possible worlds that speakers take to be live options, which do not vary from participant to participant.

At a pragmatic level of analysis, then, the defeasibility problem in presupposition can be overcome by employing linguistic procedures that represent textual contents that call for access to the lexical properties of terms, the previously represented contents in the discourse context itself, and the deictic context of utterances. But this still leaves unsolved the projection problem in presupposition.

Fortunately, Gazdar (1979) provides potential analysts with a set of procedures that correctly predict the defeat of presuppositions, even in cases where presuppositional compositionality fails to hold. Gazdar suggests that one identifies all the *possible* presuppositions of a sentence, no matter the defeasibility or projection concerns. Once the actual assertion is represented, one can then enter its entailments, followed by its conversational implicatures. Only then can one employ a canceling mechanism to determine the plausible presuppositions, eliminating those presuppositions that are logically inconsistent with the discourse as represented. Whatever survives is then added to the representation. In essence, an analyst must mark the representations of presuppositions so that they can be retracted if, later in the discourse, they are contradicted by assertional contents.

Gazdar's procedures are framed in terms of the individual speaker. Put differently, the actual presuppositions are those members of the set of possible presuppositions that are consistent with what a speaker has previously asserted, entailed, implicated, and presupposed. Levinson (1983:212n) suggests that Gazdar's procedures can be extended to what discourse participants jointly presume, as called for by Stalnaker's definition of pragmatic presupposition quoted in (32).

Contexts of the Discourses of the Three National Anthems

The story behind the African National Anthem requires retelling. The South African Enoch Mankayi Sontanga composed what later became the African National Anthem, *Nkosi Sikelel'i Afrika*, in 1897. This song was composed at a time when Africans in South Africa were living in a period of high political expectation. The song is a product of the politico-religious movement of the time, which took the form of the religion of the oppressed, and became the ideological expression of the progressive tendencies of the anti-colonial resistance (Meli 1988:32).

The composer, Sontanga, who was born in Lovedale, Cape Province, in 1860, left school at an early age and went to live in Johannesburg. A devout Christian, endowed with a wonderful voice, Sontanga wrote both the words and the music to the song. *Nkosi Sikelela* was publicly sung for the first time in 1899 at the ordination of the Reverend M. Bowemi, a Methodist priest. The occasion was said to have been marked with joy, but the composition itself was inspired by a somewhat melancholy strain: Africans were far from being happy at the height of the Anglo-Boer War (Meli 1988:32).

Sontanga died in 1904, but African teachers and poets such as J. L. Dube (who later became the African National Congress [ANC] President-General), R. T. Caluza, and S. E. K. Mqhayi popularized the song. The song was originally intended as a hymn, but it began to be sung in schools and churches in all provinces and developed an adaptation acknowledging the unity of the African people. On January 8, 1912, it was sung at the birth of the ANC; and in 1925, the ANC adopted it as its national anthem. Today, adapted forms of the song serve as national anthems for Namibia, Tanzania, Zambia, and Zimbabwe (Meli 1988:32-33).

The Jamaican National Anthem was written in 1962 to commemorate the country's independence from Great Britain. The Hon. The Rev. Hugh B. Sherlock, OJ, OBE, JP, DD, LLD, MIBA, wrote the lyrics to the anthem and the Hon. Robert Charles Lightbourne, OJ, wrote the music (Jamaican Government Public Relations Office n.d., n.p.).

Sherlock was Minister of Religion, served as a consultant for the Intercontinental Biography, served as Chairman of Boys Town All-Age, and served as Chairman of Boys Town Finance Committee. Born in Portland, Jamaica, on March 21, 1905, he was the son of the late Rev. Terrence M. Sherlock and Adina Trotter-Sherlock. He was educated at Beckford and Smith's School, Calabar High School, Caenwood Methodist Theological College in Jamaica, and was ordained in 1937 (Jamaican Government Public Relations Office n.d.:228).

Lightbourne was Chairman and Managing Director of Textiles of Jamaica, Ltd. and served as Vice-President of the Jamaican Olympic Association. Born in Morant Bay, Jamaica, on November 29, 1909, he was the son of the late Robert Augustus Lightbourne, Minister and Politician. He was educated at Jamaica College and in England (Jamaican Government Public Relations Office n.d.:181).

The period in which the Jamaican National Anthem was written was one of hardship for the country. Jamaica faced a high inflation rate, a high unemployment rate, and massive poverty. Many citizens were dissatisfied, and their discontent sometimes led to riots and violent crime. Some Jamaicans supported Black Power groups that called for more African Jamaican control over the economy and the government. The Black Power groups also urged the government to nationalize the bauxite and alumina industries, which were largely controlled by foreign companies (Singham and Singham 1976:11:23).

Lift Ev'ry Voice and Sing was written in 1901 by James Weldon Johnson (1871-1938). He was a novelist, playwright, and poet (Brooks 1984:179). He pursued his studies through a collegiate course and emerged as a major voice in public affairs and one of the major authors of his time. Johnson served as Spence Professor of Creative Literature at Fisk University. He translated the libretto of Enrique Granados' opera, Goyescas, which was written by Fernando Periquet, from Spanish to English to be presented at the Metropolitan Opera House in New York (Cuney-Hare 1936/1974:167, 169).

Johnson inaugurated New York's Harlem Renaissance movement with the publication of his *Fifty Years and Other Poems* in 1917. The movement, which became the centerpiece of African American intellectual life, was an outcome of the disillusionment of African Americans concerning their plight in the United States after World War I. They became increasingly aware that the democracy for which they had fought and some of their brothers had died in Europe did not exist for them in America. Thus, they became more militant and more articulate in expressing their displeasures about their economic and social conditions (Brooks 1984:203).

Between 1901 and the late 1920s, *Lift Ev'ry Voice and Sing* had emerged as a national patriotic hymn sung for African Americans. It was greatly appreciated for its melodically beautiful production and tremendous racial and national appeal, and was widely used by African American organizations all over the United States (Cuney-Hare 1936/1974:169).

From the 1930s to the early 1950s, however, African American colleges discouraged the singing of what was long regarded as the Negro National Hymn, *Lift Ev'ry Voice and Sing*. As Branch (1988:137-138) has pointed out, a few African American college presidents even forbade the singing of the hymn. At some institutions, teachers, students, and administrators objected to the inclusion of the spirituals in the repertoires of their college choirs. The reason for this, according to Branch, was that many of the African American teachers and administrators had received their graduate training at White Northern universities. Therefore, the thrust of the educational programs of the colleges was towards preparing students to eventually take their 'rightful places' in the mainstream of American culture. As a result, most members of the college communities, including the students, felt that the proper avenue for entering the mainstream was assimilation into White culture.

In sum, the three national anthems were written by Africans who were brilliant, religious, spiritual, and had a positive world-view, despite their travails and those of their people. All three anthems were written during very trying times for the people of the African Diaspora. That the triangle of shame—i.e. Africans from the continent being enslaved and taken to the Caribbean and then some of them to the Americas—did not destroy the fundamental ontology of Africans is quite evident here.

Analysis: Presuppositions of the Anthems

The three anthems read as follows:

African National Anthem

>Nkosi Sikelel'i Afrika
>Maluphakanisw' upondo lwayo
>Yizwa imitandazo yetu
>Usi—sikelele
>
>Sikelel' amadol' asizwe
>Sikelela kwa nomlisela
>Ulitwal' ilizwe ngomonde
>Uwusikilele
>
>Sikelel' amalinga etu
>Awonanyana nokuzaka
>Awemfundo nemvisiswano
>Uwasikelele
>
>Woza Moya! [Yihla] Moya!
>Woza Moya Oyingcwele!
>
>God bless Africa
>Raise up her spirit
>Hear our prayers
>And bless us

Bless the leaders
Bless also the young
That they may carry the land with patience
And that you may bless them

Bless our efforts
To unite and lift ourselves up
Through learning and understanding
And bless them

Come Spirit! [Descend] Spirit!
Come, Holy Spirit!

Jamaican National Anthem

Eternal Father bless our land,
Guard us with They Mighty Hand
Keep us free from evil powers,
Be our light through countless hours.
To our Leaders Great Defender,
Grant true wisdom from above.
Justice, Truth be ours forever,
Jamaica, Land we love.
Jamaica, Jamaica, Jamaica land we love.

Teach us true respect for all,
Stir response to duty's call,
Strengthen us the weak to cherish,
Give us vision lest we perish.
Knowledge send us Heavenly Father,
Grant true wisdom from above.
Justice, Truth be ours forever,
Jamaica, land we love.
Jamaica, Jamaica, Jamaica land we love.

Negro National Anthem

Lift ev'ry voice and sing
Till earth and heaven ring,
Ring with the harmonies of liberty;
Let our rejoicing rise High as the listening skies,
Let it resound loud as the rolling sea.
Sing a song full of the faith that the dark past has taught us,
Sing a song full of the hope that the present has brought us,
Facing the rising sun of our new day begun
Let us march on till victory is won.

Stony the road we trod,
Bitter the chastening rod,
Felt in the days when hope unborn had died.
Yet with a steady beat,
Have not our weary feet
Come to the place for which our fathers sighed?
We have come over a way that with tears has been watered,
We have come, treading our path through the blood of the
    slaughtered, Out from the gloomy past,
Till now we stand at last
Where the white gleam of our bright star is cast.

God of our weary years,
God of our silent tears,
Thou who hast brought us thus far on the way;
Thou who hast by Thy might
Led us into the light,
Keep us forever in the path, we pray.
Lest our feet stray from the places, our God, where we met
    Thee,
Lest our hearts drunk with the wine of the world, we forget
    Thee; Shadowed beneath Thy hand,

May we forever stand.

True to our God, True to our native land.

It is quite evident from the text of the African National Anthem that all the presupposition triggers[9] in that text are *performative verbs/predicates* or what Karttunen (1973:174) refers to as *plugs*: bless, raise up, hear, carry, unite, lift up, and come/descend. From the Jamaican National Anthem, it can be seen that all the presupposition triggers are also *performatives*: bless, guard, keep free, be, grant, love, teach, stir, strengthen, give, and send. What is common to these verbs is that they are used to report on what illocutionary acts (in the sense of Austin 1962) are to be performed. As Karttunen (1973:174) observes, one can report that a certain illocutionary act has taken place (in the texts of the African National Anthem and the Jamaican National Anthem, that certain illocutionary acts are to take place) without thereby committing oneself to the presuppositions of whatever was said or written on that occasion. For all the stretches of discourses in the texts of these two anthems (the African and the Jamaican), then, the complement sentences have presuppositions which are not presuppositions for the main sentences. (It is assumed here that infinitival and gerundive clauses originate as complete sentences in the underlying syntactic representation. Nothing important hinges on this assumption, as Karttunen correctly points out.)

From the Negro National Anthem, several types of presupposition triggers can be identified. The majority of these, however, are performatives: lift, ring, let rise, let resound, sing, keep, come, pray, stray, forget, and stand true.

A significant number of the presupposition triggers are *factives*: facing, trod, felt, out, led, drunk, and is won. Factive verbs/predicates as presupposition triggers carry along the writer's propositions that the complement sentences of the statement represent true propositions. Automatic recognition of such propositions presents no particular problem, as syntactic triggers (the presence of undefeated factive predicates) plainly appear in the pertinent statements in the text of the Negro National Anthem.

Many of the presupposition triggers are *definite descriptions*: the dark past, the present, our new day, the chastening rod, steady beat, our weary feet, our bright star, God of our weary years, thy might, and our hearts. As presupposition triggers, definite descriptions, according to Russell (1905), have nothing like the simple logical translation that we might imagine. Although they occur in natural language as subjects, in logical form they are not logical subjects at all but correspond instead to conjunctions of propositions. Thus, by virtue of the Russellian expansion of the phrases from which this type of propositions are embedded, it can be asserted that the writer of the Negro National Anthem noticed, for example, that "there was a dark past" and "there is a present (time)."

A small number of the presupposition triggers are *change of state predicates*: have come, and has brought. Change of state predicates as presupposition triggers appear in conditionals which have all the presuppositions that their antecedents and consequents have independently. This signifies that the author of the Negro National Anthem did not want to commit himself to certain false beliefs for which he had no concrete evidence. In semantic terms, the bivalence of a sentence does not depend on whether the proposition of the complement is true.

Thus, the following presuppositions can be derived from the text of the African National Anthem:

(33) God blesses, raises up spirits, and listens.

(34) The young carry the land.

(35) Unity and lifting up oneself hinge on learning and understanding.

(36) Spirits come/descend.

From the text of the Jamaican National Anthem, the following presuppositions can be suggested:

(37) God blesses, guards, keeps people free, serves as a light, grants true wisdom to leaders, teaches, stirs responses, strengthens the weak, gives vision, and sends knowledge.

(38) Utterers want justice and truth.

(39) Jamaicans are loving people.

For the Negro National Anthem, many presuppositions can be suggested as follows:

(40) There are many voices.

(41) There is an earth and a heaven.

(42) Liberty is harmonious.

(43) There is rejoicing.

(44) There are listening skies.

(45) There is a rolling sea.

(46) There is a song full of faith.

(47) There was a dark past.

(48) There is a song full of hope.

(49) There is a present time.

(50) There is a rising sun.

(51) There is a new day.

(52) Victory can be won.

(53) There was a road.

(54) There was a chastening rod.

(55) There was no hope.

(56) There was a steady beat.

(57) Utterers' feet were weary.

(58) There was a place where utterers' fathers sighed.

(59) There were tears.

(60) There was blood of the slaughtered.

(61) There was a gloomy past.

(62) There was a bright star.

(63) There is a God.

(64) There is a way.

(65) God has might.

(66) There was light.

(67) There is a path.

(68) There were places God was met.

(69) Utterers have hearts.

(70) There is the wine of the world.

(71) Utterers can forget God.

(72) God has a hand.

(73) Utterers have a God.

(74) Utterers have a native land.

In sum, 42 presuppositions are identified in the texts of the three national anthems: four in the African National Anthem, three in the Jamaican National Anthem, and 35 in the Negro National Anthem. The break down of these propositions in terms of their types of presupposition triggers are presented in Table 1.

Table 1: Presupposition Triggers in the Three National Anthems

Type of Trigger	African National Anthem N %	Jamaican National Anthem N %	Negro National Anthem N %
Change of State Predicates	- -	- -	3 8%
Factive Predicates	- -	- -	9 26%
Performative Predicates	4 100%	3 100%	14 40%
Definite Descriptions	- -	- -	9 26%
Total	**4 100%**	**3 100%**	**35 100%**

As the data for the types of presupposition triggers for the texts of the three national anthems, summarized in Table 1, reveal, the largest proportion of these triggers comprises performative predicates. Reasonably larger proportions of them are factive predicates and definite descriptions; a smaller proportion is made up of change of state predicates.

These presupposition triggers carry propositions of some necessary and sufficient conditions which determine whether the events described in the texts of the three anthems took place. The writers' main statements can, thus, be looked upon as statements about whether the decisive conditions they (the writers) envisioned for generating the texts were fulfilled, and under what spatial and temporal circumstances.

This is good to know because these presupposition triggers indicate the sort of range of presuppositional phenomena the authors of the texts had. This set of core phenomena makes it possible for the examination of some further basic properties that the authors' presuppositions exhibit. In essence, while it is important to know the presuppositions of the three national anthems, it is equally important to explore explanations of why the given presuppositions are present in the texts. This will allow for a systematic and an empirical analysis of those antecedent factors that are responsible for the suggestions of these presuppositions.

Understanding the Presuppositions in the Text

The presuppositions identified in the texts of the three national anthems can be grouped within the following content categories in terms of their subject matter:

(a) God/Lord: (33), (37), (63), (65), (68), (71), (72), (73).

(b) The Young: (34).

(c) Unity and Strength: (35).

(d) Spirits: (36).

(e) Liberty, Justice, and Truth: (38), (42).

(f) Love and Joy: (39), (43), (56), (69), (70).

(g) Numericalism: (40).

(h) Earth and Heaven: (41).

(i) Faith and Hope: (46), (48), (51), (52), (53), (62), (64), (66), (67), (74).

(j) Ecological Concern: (44), (45), (50).

(k) Temporal Sequence: (49).

(l) Suffering: (47), (54), (55), (57), (58), (59), (60), (61).

While the presuppositions delineated for the three national anthems are important in knowing the core of the phenomena in the texts, they do not, however, present us with explanations for understanding the anthems. Explanations of the presupposition content categories are, therefore, imperative because any social scientific endeavor must seek to provide general explanations to "Why?" questions. In this case, the question is why the preceding presupposition categories are evident in the texts examined. When social scientists attempt to explain why a given phenomenon took place, they must provide a systematic and empirical analysis of those antecedent factors in the given situation that made possible the occurrence of that phenomenon.

God/Lord

The African notion that God[10] blesses (that is, the gift of divine favor) is derived from the belief of a supreme being as an integral part of the world-view and practiced religion of Africans. The nature of God in African belief is evident from the qualities attributed to him/her. That God is almighty (as the Temne of Sierra Leone say, *Kuru Masheba*) is one of the most obvious assertions, since supremacy calls for it. As Parrinder (1969:39-40) points out,

> All-powerful is a common name for him (her) and he (she) receives many similar titles: creator, allotter, giver of rain and sunshine, the one who began the forest, the one 'who gives the rots', maker of souls, father (mother) of the placenta, the one who exists by himself (herself). The omnipresence of God, less commonly expressed, is found in sayings such as 'the one who is met everywhere', and 'the great ocean whose head-dress is the horizon'. More clearly God is omniscient: the wise one, the all-seeing, the 'one who brings round the season'. (The feminine attributes in parentheses are mine to indicate that some African cultures have no gender markers for God and some ascribe a feminine gender to God.)

These attributes suggest the transcendence and immanence of God. As such, s/he is in a position to *bless* persons, places, things, and ideas.

The African belief that God raises up one's spirit (that is, vivacity, courage, vigor, enthusiasm, etc.) when a person encounters misfortune, sickness, barrenness, quarrels, drought, and any disruption of normal life is manifested in sacrifices of propitiation. Prayers, petitions, and praises all seek augmentation of force by recognizing and invoking the powers of the supreme being. Great endeavors are, therefore, made by Africans to 'get up,' improve and modernize their lot to become successful because they believe that God has not fixed an order that can never change or placed people in positions where they are doomed to stay (Parrinder 1969:72-73).

The sonorous rehearsals of divine qualities attributed to God in African prayers are all geared toward the belief that s/he listens to them. The Yoruba of Nigeria, for example, begin many prayers with such praise names: *Olorun, Olodumare, Baba, Alaanu Julo*; God, Almighty, Father, Most Merciful.

Faith in God, however, implies his/her providence. Thus, the poetry of African prayer, delightful as it is in expressive words, is not allowed to deviate from practical purpose. This prayer of the Kikuyu in Kenya is a case in point: "You who make mountains tremble and rivers flood; we offer you this sacrifice so that you may bring us rain. People and children are crying. We beseech you to accept this sacrifice and bring us prosperity" (Parrinder 1969:67-68). All such African prayers are believed to be heard by God who helps his/her suppliant by an intervention, either open or hidden, but powerful and effective.

Before their arrival to the New World, the belief in the existence of God/Lord among those Africans was firmly in place. As Parrinder (1969:39) has observed, the earlier view that African religions were crudely fetishistic, with an idea of God where s/he existed being an importation, has long been replaced by the view that most Africans have had the belief in a Supreme Being as an integral part of their world-view and practiced religion long before the arrival of the White man. Missionaries found, often to their surprise, that they did not need to convince Africans about the existence of God, or faith in a life after death, for both these fundamentals of world religions were deeply rooted in Africa before their arrival.

The nature of God in African belief was evident from the qualities attributed to him/her. That God is almighty is one of the most obvious assertions, since supremacy calls for it (Parrinder 1969:39).

For Africans, God possessed the power to heal mental and physical illness. S/he resided in heaven; was the creator of everything on earth: the sun, moon, sky, air, water, plants, humans, animals, etc. S/he was perceived as the benevolent mother, or father, who rewarded goodness but ruthlessly punished evil. S/he knew all, saw all, and was both omnipotent and omnipresent (Hull 1972:131).

In Jamaica, *Kumina*, regarded as the most African of Jamaican religions, was carried there by a large number of free Africans who arrived there in the 1840s to 1860s. Many of them settled in St. Thomas, where the religion is the strongest. A religion of Bantu origin, *Kumina* has been shown to be largely Ki-Kongo in present day Congo (Senior 1983:91).

In America, Gullah African Christianity was a vital folk religion, filled with patterns of beliefs linking worshipers with their traditional past. Gullah original interpretation of religion included treating spirituality as a means of communal harmony, solidarity, and accountability. These features of an African world-view, an African theory of being, and some African customs sometimes superseded, sometimes coexisted with the Christian influence. This was consonant with the notion that in a cohesive and integrated society, each member had a place (Holloway 1990:71).

For the Gullah, God, personified as Jesus, and an African world-view offered them an explanation for life and provided a model of virtue. This belief inspired them to hold on to their faith that freedom on earth would come to them in their progeny (Holloway 1990:71).

In St. Augustine, East Florida, African religious patterns exerted continuing influence among Blacks as African naming practices persisted during the era of British control (1763-1784). Another characteristic of black religious life in Florida was the high emotionalism prevalent in traditional African worship (Holloway 1990:101, 111).

The Young

In efforts to prepare African youths to take their places in family life, community affairs, and government, African children mingle with adults in the beginning of their lives sharing in ceremonies and feasts at home, in working the fields and visiting the markets, and in watching tribunals and funerals. Traditionally, many African societies were divided into age grades, and in adolescence the grade would pass through common ceremonies and initiations (such as the *Poro* for boys and *Sande* for girls in Sierra Leone and Guinea, and *Kumina* in Jamaica) into adulthood.

As Vlahos (1967:192-193) notes, the system of age grouping was one means for organizing large numbers of people from different areas. For various Nilotic ethnic groups, age grouping represented the beginning of government beyond pure family rule. Among the Zulu and Swazi of Southern Africa, age grouping served as a military complex from which government is formed. Among the Kikuyu, age grouping was the system of the whole government. Its leaders were selected not by birth, not by election, not even by divine appointment. Instead, Kikuyu leaders were chosen by the accumulation of birthdays. A government formed by "committee," every Kikuyu could hope to stand at least once in the limelight and, with his "committee" members, to orchestrate communal policy.

Politics in such a fundamental situation, according to Awoonor (1990:3), defined duties and responsibilities alongside obligations and rights. This survival concept is ever-changing, continuing, and dialectical.

Unity and Strength

That the prerequisites of unity and strength to lift up oneself in Africa hinge on one's ability to learn during his/her youth from his/her playmates and live with them is hardly a matter of dispute. The Nyakyusa of Tanzania, for instance, once lived in three villages in one: a village for the family persons, a village for the persons who ran things, and a village for their children who were learning to be adults (Vlahos 1967:210).

The Nyakyusa used to divide their interests and activities almost equally between farming and herding. A boy began taking his father's cattle to pasture when he turned six. He did not go out alone, but in a small troop of boys his own age and a little older. Cooking their own food, wrestling and fighting to see which one was the strongest, the Nyakyusa youths acknowledged the leader of all, the one whose order would be followed. When the Nyakyusa boy came home to his mother's meal, he brought his friends along and, like a swarm of locusts, they descended on one mother's larder after another (Vlahos 1967:202). The case of the Nyakyusa typifies the closeness and dependence of African youths on one another, because, even in a time of change, they still value above all things the togetherness, of comradeship and harmony.

The history of the skillful and resilient Captain Kojo who worked to unite his fellow Maroons to resist Spanish and English domination in Jamaica is well documented. Kojo was a member of a group of enslaved runaways who roamed the Clarendon hills (near Cave Valley) in the 1tth Century. He emerged as the leader and welded together all the Clarendon Maroon bands. So great did his fame become that many Maroons made their way from other parts of Jamaica to serve under his leadership (Senior 1983:91).

African Americans were (and continue to be) quite strong in order to survive. They had to endure political, social, and economic intimidation, supplemented by violence and the threat of violence. As to be discussed later, they were the victims of violence even before they began to participate in the political process. The violence intensified during the Reconstruction era. Terrorist organizations like the Ku Klux Klan, the Knights of the White Camelia, the Pale Faces, the White Line, the Knights of the Rising Sun, the White Brotherhood, the Red Shirts, and many others whipped and murdered African Americans and their White sympathizers.

As early as the presidential campaign of 1868, Whites in the Louisiana parishes of Opelousas, Caddo, and Bouvier systematically "hunted down" and killed over 400 African Americans within a month. Later that year in Moore County, North Carolina, the Ku Klux Klan murdered an African American woman and all five of her children while in the process of terrorizing African Americans and White Republicans. The violence was so widespread that Congress was moved to pass the Enforcement Acts of 1870 and 1871 to crush it (Arnold Taylor 1976:25).

Having occurred in the North during the Civil War, race riots became rampant throughout America. The South saw its share of race riots beginning with the era of Reconstruction in order to keep the African American population cowed and subordinate. Riots occurred in New Orleans and Memphis as early as 1866: in the former city, the riots were caused by White resentment of African

American demands for the suffrage; in the latter city, the rescue of an African American male by a group of African American soldiers from the custody of the police led to the riot. Other major riots included those in Meridian, Mississippi, in 1871; in Savannah, Georgia, in 1872; and in Hamburg and Charleston, South Carolina, in 1786. African Americans in Charleston, however, angry over many indignities, became the aggressors (Arnold Taylor 1976:25).

African American resistance to and retaliation against violence directed at them was commonplace. Groups of African Americans responded by patrolling the streets of Wilmington, North Carolina, for four days armed with such weapons as guns and fence rails when the Conservative White press and other elements in the city attempted to create a scare in April of 1868 in order to discourage Blacks from voting on the drafted state constitution. This demonstration forced the Ku Klux Klan to disappear from the Wilmington area for the remainder of the Reconstruction period. During the same month, a group of about 200 African Americans in Alexandria, Louisiana, armed with clubs, routed Klansmen who had been parading throughout the community and threatening to kill any African American who dared to vote on that state's constitution. Also on the night of July 4, 1868, between 20 and 30 African Americans in Columbia, Tennessee, where the Ku Klux Klan was quite entrenched, attacked a group of about 250 Klan members (Arnold Taylor 1976:25-26).

Between the end of Reconstruction and the inauguration of apartheid, African Americans continued to resist or retaliate against White violence. Democratic fraud at the polls also occasionally evoked a violent reaction from African Americans. Nonetheless, physical atrocities against African Americans, such as beatings and lynchings, provoked African American resistance and retaliation than fraud at the polls or other forms of chicanery practiced by Whites. Such crimes by Whites moved even the relatively conservative African American leaders to endorse violent responses (Arnold Taylor 1976:62-63).

During the 20th Century, many African American leaders endorsed the principle of individual and collective use of violence in self-defense. For example, W. E. B. Du Bois on many occasions between 1905 and 1935 endorsed not only the use of violence in self-defense, but prophesized a war between the races. Even the more moderate James Weldon Johnson, while rejecting the use of violence as a weapon to dismantle the racial order, nevertheless, declared in 1934 that faced with mob violence African Americans must give up their lives to resist it. In 1925, the National Association for the Advancement of Colored People (NAACP) argued and won the same principle in the Ossian Sweet case (Arnold Taylor 1976:63).

By the 1950s, militant self-defense became as much a part of the African American protest tradition as demonstrations, boycotts, litigation, petitions, and appeals to the sense of justice of Americans. The willingness of Robert Williams of Monroe, North Carolina, in the late 1950s and the Deacons for Defense in Louisiana in the 1960s to take up arms to defend their African American communities reflected an impulse that was deeply rooted in the African American Southern experience (Arnold Taylor 1976:65).

From the landing of the first enslaved Africans in Jamestown, Virginia, in August of 1619, one year before the Mayflower's arrival, until their freedom was finally granted, 250 years elapsed. African Americans were able to survive these two hundred and fifty years of anxiety, frustration, and hardship because of their mental and physical stamina that would not permit the concession of defeat.

Spirits

In order to understand the idea behind the presupposition that Spirits[11] come/descend, it is important to begin by discussing the notion of Spirits within the African context. Gods and ancestors are regarded generally as Divinity or Spiritual Activity. For Africans, however, these terms do not suggest a separation from man, or an opposition of spiritual and material, or sacred and secular. Instead, gods are regarded as being dependent on the Supreme Being, and that all powers, divine and human, are interrelated. In essence, even humans are considered Spirits (Parrinder 1969:47).

Many African myths, thus, suggest that having created the world and having lived here in olden days, God retired to the heavens where s/he is now. In order to solicit his/her help, then, s/he needs to be summoned to come/descend.

The Yoruba say that Ol-orun, 'owner of the sky,' lives in heaven with other divinities. Below was a waste marsh with no solid ground, where divinities came down to play and hunt. The Mende of Sierra Leone say that God was formerly nearer to humans than s/he is now, and s/he gave them everything they requested. But humans troubled God so often that s/he decided to go far away into the heavens. Similar themes have been documented to exist in Ivory Coast, Ghana, Togo, Dahomey, Nigeria, Sudan, Burundi, Zambia, Congo, and Kenya (Parrinder 1969:30-33). The presupposition that Spirits come/descend hinges, thus, on the notion of the creation and the separation of humans and God.

For members of the *Kumina* religion in Jamaica, singing, dancing, and drumming are the three most important elements in their session. The drums are the most important for the controls they exercise over certain kinds of spirits. Leaders have to serve long apprenticeships before attaining the highest position in the group. Leaders can be women or men. The spirits are originally of three ranks: (1) sky gods, (2) earthbound gods, and (3) ancestral spirits.

Liberty, Justice, and Truth

As Spencer (1990:35-44) has suggested, no other sentiment has inspired African Americans to exalted strains as the love of liberty. He added that there existed among African Americans a deep consciousness of the injustices of slavery and a due appreciation of the blessings of freedom, which gave rise to many anti-slavery songbooks.

Witvliet (1987) also has argued that the history of the African American struggle for liberation is deeply rooted in the belief that one's own liberation is related to that of the other. This notion, he pointed out, is evident from the following spiritual:

> You say the Lord has set you free, ...
> Why don't you let yo' neighbour be! (Witvliet 1987:18)

An examination of a number of historical records reveals that a variety of approaches were utilized by African Americans to free a fortunate minority of the enslaved from bondage. Manumission, escape, and philanthropy were all used in efforts to secure liberty for enslaved individuals and their families (see, for example, the many stories in Foner 1970).

Many of the enslaved received their liberty through military and naval service in the colonial wars and the American Revolution. Another source of freedom was self-purchase. Generally, the enslaved were able to buy their liberty used their special trade skills to hire themselves out. Some of the enslaved obtained their monies to buy their freedom in unique ways: the self-taught George Moses Horten sold his love lyrics to students at the state university of North Carolina; Denmark Vesey and Newport Gardner used their winnings from the Rhode Island lottery—the former in 1782, the latter in 1791; James Derham, a male nurse, medical assistant, and apothecary in New Orleans saved money from his services to buy his freedom in 1783, becoming an outstanding physician within six years. Derham then moved to Philadelphia, repeated his success, and won the respect of his colleagues in the medical profession (Quarles 1964:83-85).

Still, other enslaved Africans sought liberty through rebellion, albeit not always successful. For example, five enslaved Africans joined John Brown and 14 of his followers in their attempt to seize a government arsenal in Harpers Ferry in northwestern Virginia. Brown's plan failed mainly because it was staged in an area where there were few enslaved Africans and had given them no foreknowledge of his plan of attack. Consequently, Brown and his 21 men were captured and executed, leading the soldiers in blue to sing "John Brown's Body" (Quarles 1964:108). In 1793, when African-born Angolans rose up against their Carolina masters, enslaved Africans from that region were no longer so desirable. Also, a nonimportation act was put in effect for ten years following the 1793 Stono Rebellion (Holloway 1990:69). The three greatest slave revolts in American history occurred within the space of 31 years during the 19th Century. The first was led by a 24-year-old enslaved African in Virginia, Gabriel, in 1800. Gabriel devised a plan for three columns of armed slaves to attack Richmond, seize the arsenal, and kill all the Whites, except Quakers, Methodists, and Frenchmen. Before Gabriel could regroup, the militia had been alerted and he and 25 of his men were captured and executed. Denmark Vesey, an enslaved carpenter in Charleston who won enough money in a lottery to buy his freedom, began organizing for an armed insurrection among slaves in Charleston and the surrounding countryside. Vesey's plot, however, was betrayed by a privileged enslaved African, leading to Vesey's execution. Nat Turner's rebellion occurred ten years after Vesey was executed. Turner's uprising was the last major revolt which got beyond the planning stage. He had no grand plan, and started out with only a handful of followers. His life revolved around religion, conducting religious services among the enslaved Africans in Southampton County, Virginia. Between 1828 and 1830, Turner saw visions and spirits which he interpreted as divine instructions to lead the revolt. Turner and his men killed about 60 Whites before being captured and killed (Foner 1970:113-115).

The Gullah, especially, were extremely courageous. Their men, women, and children risked their lives in the pursuit of freedom when the Union Army occupied part of South Carolina. They did not only survive, they taxed their creative talents to develop their own community (Holloway 1990:76).

In their call for total emancipation, African Americans became active participants in newspaper work, owning and managing twenty-four periodicals during the 30 years after the Civil War (1861-1865). These African American newspapers were not the official mouthpiece of the abolitionist societies, but fully supported the crusade. Although some encountered financial difficulties, they still managed to publish a few series. The common devotion of these periodicals to the principles of liberty and equality was underscored by some of their titles—*Freedom's Journal, The Rights of All, Mirror of Liberty, Impartial Citizen,* and *Herald of Freedom* (Quarles 1964:106-107).

As John Taylor (1975:398) observed, it is to the enslaved African's credit that s/he refused to lapse into a permanent state of docility; and that even though s/he was occasionally forced to cope with the aggressive feelings toward Whites by means of defense mechanisms, s/he nevertheless was determined to use his/her limited resources to seek his/her liberty. This determination, according to Taylor, spilled over into the white people's consciousness and emancipation eventually followed.

Joy and Love

Before they were brought to the shores of the New World, the Africans had expressed themselves musically in all life situations. Likewise, in America and in the Caribbean the various generations of enslaved Africans used songs to accompany menial labor, learn facts, vent their frustrations, share religion, and relate their life conditions. The song served as a master index to the mind of the enslaved African (John Taylor 1975:387).

The enslaved were able to develop a means of ingenious covert expression which was their own through their songs. Using the Judeo-Christian vocabulary, they attached secondary meanings, images and concepts to the song texts. They were able to harbor and express thoughts indiscernible to outsiders by developing this type of communication. Not understanding what the enslaved were doing, Whites poked fun at them for using such unintelligible jargon. In order to preserve for themselves a degree of intellectual freedom, the enslaved endured this ridicule (John Taylor 1975:387).

As John Taylor (1975:389) has pointed out, the "happy songs" were means used by the enslaved to make themselves happy, not of expressing happiness. Indeed, there was nothing glamorous about being an enslaved person that could make the individual happy. A matter of fact, many songs openly expressed despair, frustration, and sorrow.

Numericalism

Mazrui (1977:247) has defined "numericalism" as an aspect of inter-group relation describing the collection of attitudes or general principles which assign a moral premium on numerical advantage. He distinguished the range of forms which numericalism manifests: from the moral complexities of 'majority rule' to the simple belief that 'there is strength in numbers.' The two ideas, he added, do not necessarily amount to the same thing, but that they could indeed overlap. The liberal concept of majority rule rests on the idea that those who prevail in numbers are to dominate in politics. The notion of 'strength in numbers,' on the other hand, could be called upon even in situations in which majority rule as an elaborate system of government is not in favor. Even in situations where the power of numbers is seen in physical terms, numericalism still hinges on the belief that there is dignity in being numerous.

For African Americans, there have been many occasions when the more militant among them saw the significance of their numbers in quasi-military terms. Even during slavery, African American superiority in individual situations occasionally turned an African American's thought towards a possible rebellion. In situations where it did not lead to rebellion, this was sometimes interpreted by African American militants as a sign of servility. A defiant and religious African American who had lived close to slavery in North Carolina, David Walker, for example, put it this way in 1829:

> Here now, in the Southern and Western Sections of this country (United States) there are at least three coloured persons for one white, why is it that those few weak, good-for-nothing whites are able to keep so many able men ... in wretchedness and misery? It shows what the blacks are, we are ignorant, abject, servile and mean—and the whites know it—they know that we are servile to assert our rights as men—or they would not fool with us as they do (1829/1965:129).

Walker went on to add:

> O Americans! Americans!! I call God—I call angels—I call men, to witness that your DESTRUCTION is at hand, and will be speedily consummated unless you REPENT (1829/1905:129).

In contemporary times, the African American population has come to perceive the significance of its size more in electoral terms instead of in revolutionary ones. African Americans have come to link their size with the liberating potential of the franchise. The African American historian, Aptheker, for example, captured this sentiment quite well when he stated:

> It never was right 'for the administration' to 'postpone' effective action on the Negro question because of so-called political expediency; to say it is not wrong, it is unwise.... President Kennedy would have remained a United States Senator if but 75 per cent of the Negro vote went his way in 1960 rather than the 85 per cent cast for him (1964:109).

A similar observation has been made by contemporary African American leaders about the importance of the African American vote in presidential elections. Many have asserted that the African American vote has made the difference in Democratic Party's electoral victories in several elections.

As Mazrui (1977:249) observed, at its more revolutionary peak, the African Americans' belief in the importance of their numbers becomes more astute. Speeches to African Americans suggesting that they reduce their rate of reproduction are widely interpreted as a device to keep them numerically weak. Mazrui also suggested that the battle cry of revolutionary African American militancy might almost be paraphrased in the following slogan: "Burn, baby, burn!—and then breed some more!" This, he believed, is a dual strategy of engaging both in destructive acts which weaken the power of the white man and in creative acts which strengthen the power of the African American. In short order, how can African Americans "lift ev'ry voice and sing," if there are not enough voices to be lifted?

Earth and Heaven

The notions of earth and heaven (or heaven and earth) were not foreign to Africans before their arrival to the New World. As Parrinder (1969:54), for example, has pointed out, when a grave is dug in the ground, a libation is made to the spirit, a custom that was taken to America and other parts of the New World by the enslaved Africans. This veneration of the earth by African Americans and Jamaicans, for example, can be traced back to a number of African cultures. Ashanti drummers address the earth in the following words:

> Earth, while I am yet alive,
> It is upon you that I put my trust ...
> We are addressing you,
> And you will understand (Parrinder 1969:54).

The powers of earth include the spirits of hills and great monuments like Mount Cameroon and Mount Kilimanjaro. Even the small hills in Ibadan, Nigeria have rituals recording the foundation of the city. A holiday is proclaimed every year when work stops and fires are extinguished till they are relit by the priest who is regarded the "worshipper of the hills." Rocks and outstanding formations are seen as centers where special power is manifested and available (Parrinder 1969:55).

Many Africans believed (and many still do) that the first users of metals descended from heaven with metal weapons and tools to clear the forest. Black-smithery is still an expert profession, and many smiths serve as priests to the god of metal (Parrinder 1969:56).

Thus, it is not surprising that John Taylor (1975:397) found, after studying earlier African American spirituals, that the enslaved held the belief of heaven being a dimension of self-extension in the sense of private possession. They believed that in heaven, there will be no proscription, no segregation, no sepa-rateness, no slave row. They also believed that there will exist the most psycholog-ically dramatic of all manifestations of freedom: that is, complete freedom of movement.

Faith and Hope

According to John Taylor (1975:392-393), one aspect of self-pity reflected in African American spirituals derived from the enslaved Africans' hope that the tables would eventually be turned on their oppressors. Put differently, the greater the suffering at the hands of the Whites in this life, the greater the victory over them in the afterlife would be. Self-pity was one way for the enslaved to resolve the crisis, not an end in itself; that although they felt sorry for themselves, and would ask others to pity them as well, they believed that they would not be ulti-mately defeated.

Another way the enslaved coped with their status was their identification with Jesus—the suffering hero. This identification was valuable to them not only because it helped them explain their position (whether unjust fate, or even the will of God), but also to avoid feelings of personal inferiority. It allowed them to experience vicariously feelings of achievement and adequacy through the figure held in great esteem by members of the master-class. Moreover, it helped them divert their hatred and resentment toward their White masters and overseers (John Taylor 1975:393-396).

Ecological Concern

That the ecological concern present in African American hymns was derived from African belief-systems is hardly a matter of dispute. As Mazrui (1977:262) has pointed out, for the African, ecological concern goes beyond mere fascination. It requires an individual to conserve and enrich, to empathize with nature, to see a little of him-/her-self and a little of his/her God in his/her surrounding. It calls for a totemic frame of reference. In this respect, ecological concern is much more deeply interlinked with fundamental aspects of African belief-systems than it is to those of Europeans (Mazrui 1977:262).

Totemism in Africa led groups to identify themselves with objects or other animals. Some clans adopted totemic symbols which established a sense of continuity between nature and man. The belief-systems of Africans did not assert a monopoly of the soul for the human species alone: trees, mountains, rivers, etc., all have souls (Mazrui 1977:267).

In America, the Gullah of South Carolina, for example, believed in spirits that include superhumans, animals, and objects without biological life. They applied the African ontology, adapted Christianity and bondage to it, and created a religion that used spirituality as a way of self-preservation and as an important component of community life (Holloway 1990:91). As previously noted, this is also true for members of the *Kumina* religion in Jamaica.

Temporal Sequence

The temporal sequence found in Jamaican and African American hymns can be traced back to traditional African belief-systems. These belief-systems link the past with the present and the future so intimately that life and death themselves become points on a continuum rather than opposite sides of the same coin.

Mazrui (1977:270) cited Professor John S. Mbiti as stating that the period after death in certain African traditional belief-systems is often divided into two parts: (1) *Sasa* (the now or the present)—an earlier period of "death within living memory," and (2) *Zamani* (the long ago)—a later period concerning "death beyond living recollection." As long as the individual is remembered by relatives and friends who knew him/her in his/her life, and who have survived him/her, s/he remains in the *Sasa* period. As long as the deceased is remembered by name, s/he is not completely dead: s/he is a member of "the living dead."

Belief in afterlife was central to traditional African religions. But Africans neither viewed the future world with fear, nor as a place for dispensations for rewards and punishments as Christians do. In this afterlife, there was no sickness, disease, poverty, or hunger. Death was a journey to the spirit world, not a divorce from life or earthly beings. Thus, the Gullah retained their West African initiation experience in their attitude towards death when they were brought to the New World. They attached tremendous significance to death, but showed no apprehension to the prospect of dying. As enslaved Africans, they lived in the presence of death constantly and seemed to feel that the phenomenon was as much a part of living as their continuous travail (Holloway 1990:81-82).

Suffering

That no other group of people in the New World has endured as much suffering as African Americans is undisputable. Thus, many African Americans reflected realistically in the spirituals upon the circumstances of their lives; and the suffering of Jesus was the most significant aspect of their identification with him. The scenes of Jesus' crucifixion particularly impressed them (John Taylor 1975:395). A full discussion of the suffering African Americans have endured in America, however, would require volumes. What follows, therefore, is only a sampling.

After their capture, enslaved Africans were taken aboard the slave ship. They were usually shackled by attaching the right wrist and ankle of one to the left wrist and ankle of another. The captives slept without covering on bare wooden floors, which were often constructed of unplaned boards. In rough seas, the skins over the elbows of the enslaved would wear away to the bare bones (Johnson and Campbell 1981:14).

The journey of the enslaved from West African coasts to the New World is frequently referred to as the *Middle Passage*: that is, the second leg of the triangular trading voyage between the continents of Europe and Africa, Africa and America, and America and Europe. "Tight packers" were by far the most frequently used for shipping the enslaved by the mid-18th Century. The potential profit on each enslaved African was so great that most captains used every possible space for the storage of human cargo (Johnson and Campbell 1981:13-14).

The discomfort of the densely packed quarters of the slave ships was wretched. The hold of a slave vessel was usually about five feet high. When rigged for "tight packing," another shelf or platform was built in the middle of it extending six feet from each side of the vessel. Another row of the enslaved was packed on the platform when the bottom of the hold was completely filled. A second platform was usually installed to hold more of the enslaved if there was as much as six feet of vertical space in the vessel. Such arrangements made it impossible for the enslaved to sit upright, since they were left with only about two feet of headroom (Johnson and Campbell 1981:14).

Diseases, death, and suicide plagued almost all voyages. Smallpox, scurvy, various forms of ophthalmia, and flux were the diseases most feared. Many slave ships lost half their "cargoes." For every enslaved African brought to America alive, many others died in warfare, along the treks leading to the West African coast, awaiting shipment, or in crowded and contaminated holds of the slaving vessels. Suicide was common on most voyages. On some vessels, it was epidemic. For example, in 1737, more than a hundred slaves reportedly jumped overboard from the *Prince of Orange* while the ship was anchored at St. Kitts (Johnson and Campbell 1981:15).

The last leg of the *Middle Passage*, which took about five weeks, was usually less restrictive. All but a few of the enslaved would be released from their iron shackles and brought to the deck for relief. This practice was not motivated by humanitarian purposes, but rather to prepare the enslaved for the market. The enslaved were given bigger meals and as much water as they could drink if the remaining stock of provisions was sufficient. Some captains would set the last day for limited frolicking in the form of costume party on deck, with the females dancing in the sailors' discarded clothing. At the final destination, the captain was rowed ashore to arrange for the sale of his involuntary passengers (Johnson and Campbell 1981:15).

While in America, the enslaved were considered by their masters as property as stipulated by law. These enslaved Africans were seen as less *human*, but still were expected to meet certain standards of behavior: obedience, fidelity, humility, docility, cheerfulness, etc. Those who failed to meet these standards received a variety of punishments that ranged from public flogging to death. Absolute power for the master meant absolute dependency for the enslaved (Foner 1970:95).

Even after the Emancipation Proclamation was signed by President Abraham Lincoln on January 1, 1863, the woes of African Americans were far from being over. Despite the seductiveness of freedom, many former enslaved Africans remained at the homesteads of their former masters. They were inspired not by affection for their old masters, but by the hope of finding some means of livelihood in familiar surroundings or among familiar people. As an assembly of African Americans in Charleston, South Carolina recognized in the fall of 1865, White prejudice was the major obstacle to real liberty (Arnold Taylor 1976:5-6).

African Americans in Charleston soon learned that not only were Whites in South Carolina disinclined to rise above their deeply ingrained prejudices, but that neither President Lincoln nor his successor, President Andrew Johnson, was in a position to envisage a place of equality and dignity for Blacks in American society. Both men believed that America was a "White man's country" and must remain that way. During the course of the Civil War, Lincoln investigated and launched projects aimed at colonizing the Africans in Haiti and other parts of Latin America. Despite his belief that the highly intelligent Africans and those who had fought on the side of the Union should be accorded the right to vote, he made no provisions for extending citizenship rights to freedmen in his plan to restore the Southern states to their "proper place" within the Union. Johnson privately suggested that the right of suffrage be extended to literate and propertied African Americans as a way of facilitating Northern acceptance of his lenient Reconstruction program. He was, however, adamantly opposed to elevating the mass of African Americans to civil and political equality in the South. Such a development, according to him, would lead to the dreaded "Africanization" of the region. Encouraged by Lincoln and Johnson's attitudes, Southern states enacted laws ("black codes") in 1865 and 1866 that came close to reinstituting the system of slavery (Arnold Taylor 1976:6).

The Lincoln and Johnson Administrations supplemented the "black codes" with restriction of suffrage and public education to whites in order to assure the subordinate status of African Americans. Many towns joined the bandwagon by passing ordinances that severely limited the social, economic and political freedoms of former enslaved Africans. Many Southern Whites were not content on legislation alone to keep freedmen in their place. The freedmen, no longer having the status of property and, as a result, no longer enjoying the protection of their former masters against physical abuse by other whites, became victims of violence. These African Americans were beaten, maimed, killed; their schools, churches and personal property were frequently ransacked and burnt (Arnold Taylor 1976:7).

During this era, the Ku Klux Klan was formed and soon emerged as the leading terrorist organization of the Reconstruction period. The activities of this organization, the "black codes," and the denial of suffrage and education to African Americans were widely endorsed by Southern Whites (Arnold Taylor 1976:8).

Freedmen who migrated to the North were not welcomed with open arms either. Northern Whites, who had shown little or no unusual hostility toward African Americans already living in their midst, were not in a mood to welcome those from the South. These newcomers were considered crude and rough. Many Whites living in the West had hoped also to keep their region free not only of slavery, but of freedmen as well (Johnson and Campbell 1981:41).

During the Antebellum period, conditions continued to deteriorate for African Americans in the North. Physical and social conditions in the 1830s were so harsh that many were convinced that African Americans would eventually be annihilated. Northern and Western Whites became more hostile as the population of African Americans continued to increase in these areas. On many occasions, the violence culminated into riots. In the 1830s and 1840s, racial riots frequently erupted in New York state, Ohio, and Pennsylvania (Johnson and Campbell 1981:41-42).

Conclusion

Evident from the preceding discussion is the fact that a significant number of African world-views has survived both on the continent and in the Diaspora. These notions have been missed by many authors writing about the African Diaspora because they fail to present a proper appraisal of the real nature of African thought, and because their works are based on a concept that fragments African life derived from a Eurocentric division of labor theory which separates original politics from religion, economics, and the social institutions of family, or group, or people. This fragmentation theory emanates from Eurocentric epistemology and a fundamental approach to existence which has its genesis in Greco-Roman and subsequently Judeo-Christian thought.

An examination of the African, Jamaican and Negro national anthems makes it abundantly clear that before we attempt any description of African thought, it is necessary for us to locate its total personality within the boundaries of its own self-perception; this means delineating African philosophy and its view of the world, both visible and invisible, its fundamental habits of thought, and its attitude towards its physical and spiritual existence. This is because the African life concept is holistic: that is, it is based on an integrative world-view. All life to the African is total; all human activities are closely interrelated. This has as its underlying principle the sanctity of the person, his/her spirituality and essentiality. This essentialist view of the person confers value to his/her personhood. All else—his/her labor and achievements—flow from this value system. Even personal failure cannot invalidate it.

As can be gleaned from the presuppositional analysis of the three national anthems, for the African, politics defines duties and responsibilities alongside obligations and rights. All these relate to the various activities that have to do with survival. The survival concept is continuing, dynamic, and dialectical. The fundamental principle that is at the basis of this conception is a moral one.

The African moral order never defined rigid frontiers of good and evil. Good and evil exist in the same continuum. Whatever is good, by the very nature of its goodness, harbors a grain of evil. This is a guarantee against any exaggerated sense of moral superiority which goodness by itself may entail. The notion of perfection, therefore, is alien to African thought. Perfection in itself constitutes a temptation to danger, an invitation to arrogance and self-glorification. The principle of balance defines the relationship between good and evil and *vice-versa*.

Endnotes

1. Presuppositions refer to background assumptions against which the main import of utterances or statements can be assessed (Levinson 1983:173).

2. The term linguistic framework as used here refers to a way of studying various aspects of human language and its interaction with other areas of human culture and behavior, which calls for collecting pertinent data concerning a range of linguistic phenomena, observing the patterns which underlie those phenomena, and expressing the observed regularities my means of certain linguistic rules.

3. According to Elder and Cobb (1983:28), "A symbol is any object used by human beings to index meanings that are not inherent in, nor discernible from, the object itself."

4. Interested readers can find greater details in Gazdar (1979) and Levinson (1983).

5. *Modus ponens* refers to the inference from p→q and ~p to ~q.

6. *Bivalence* refers to the assumption (pv~p) that a presupposition must be either true or false.

7. *Modus tollens* refers to the inference from p→q and q~ to ~p.

8. *Deictic Context* refers to the speech event in which languages encode or grammaticalize linguistic features. The traditional categories of deixis are person, place, and time (Levinson 1983:54,62). To these traditional categories, Lyons (1977) and Filmore (1968, 1975) add discourse (or text) deixis and social deixis.

9. Levinson (1983:181-185) summarizes 13 presupposition triggers: definite descriptions, factive verbs, implicative verbs, change of state verbs, iteratives, verbs of judging, temporal clauses, cleft sentences, implicit clefts with

stressed constituents, comparison and contrasts, non-restrictive relative clauses, counterfactual conditionals, and questions.

10. The earlier view that African religion was crudely fetishistic, with an idea of God where s/he existed being an importation, has long been replaced by the view that most Africans have had the belief in a Supreme Being as an integral part of their world-view and practiced religion long before the arrival of the White man. Missionaries found, often to their surprise, that they did not need to convince Africans about the existence of God, or faith in a life after death, for both these fundamentals of world religion were deeply rooted in Africa before their arrival.

11. The use of the word 'Spirit' here refers to a supernatural being of a certain (good or evil) character. This differs from the earlier use of 'spirit' (as in 'God raises up one's spirits') which refers to vivacity, courage, vigor, enthusiasm, etc.

Bibliography

Abrahams, Roger. (1968). Pull out your purse and pay. *Folklore* 79:176-201.

Achebe, Chinua. (1964). *Arrow of God*. London: Heinemann.

Adamson, Alan H. (1975). The reconstruction of plantation labor after emancipation: The case of British Guiana. In Stanley L. Engerman and Eugene D. Genovese, eds. *Race and Slavery in the Western Hemisphere: Quantitative Studies*. Princeton, NJ: Princeton University Press.

Afolabi Ojo, G. J. (1966). *Yoruba Culture: A Geographical Analysis*. London: University of London Press.

Alleyne, Mervyn. (Winter 1970). The linguistic continuity of Africa in the Caribbean. *Black Academy Review* 1:3-16.

Allsopp, Richard and Jeannette Allsop. (2003). *Dictionary of Caribbean English Usage*. Kingston, Jamaica: University of the West Indies Press.

Alvárez Nazario, Manuel. (1977). *El Influjo Indígena en el Español de Puerto Rico*. San Juan, Puerto Rico: University of Puerto Rico Press.

Alvárez Nazario, Manuel. (1967). *El Elemento Afro-negroide en el Español de Puerto Rico: Contribución al Estudio del Negro en América*. San Juan, Puerto Rico: University of Puerto Rico Press.

Ammon, Ulrich, ed. (1989). *Status and Function of Languages and Language Varieties*. Berlin and New York: Walter de Gruyter, Inc.

Anstey, Roger and A. P. Antippas. (1975). *The Atlantic Slave Trade and the British Abolition, 1760-1810*. Atlantic Highlands, NJ: Brill Academic Publishers.

Anstey, Roger. (1975). The volume and profitability of the British slave trade, 1761-1807. In Stanley L. Engerman and Eugene D. Genovese, eds. *Race and Slavery in the Western Hemisphere: Quantitative Studies*. Princeton, NJ: Princeton University Press.

Aptheker, H. (1964). *Soul of the Republic: The Negro Today*. New York: Marzani and Munsell.

Ardener, Edwin. (1959). Lineage and locality among the Mba-Ise-Ibo. *Africa* 29:113-33.

Armah, Ayi Kwei. (2006). *The Eloquence of the Scribes*. England: New African.

Asein, Samuel. (1971). The concept of form: A study of some ancestral elements in Brathwaite's trilogy. *African Studies Association of West Indies Bulletin* 4:9-38.

Asiegbu, J. (1970). *Slavery and the Politics of Liberation, 1787-1861: A Study of Liberated African Emigration and British Anti-slavery Policy*. London: Holmes and Meir Publishers.

Ata Aidoo, Ama. (September 21, 1968). Akan and English. *West Africa*.

Austin, J. L. (1962). *How to Do Things with Words*. Cambridge, Mass.: Harvard University Press.

Awoonor, K. N. (1990). *Ghana: A Political History*. Accra: Sedco Publishing Ltd. and Woeli Publishing Service.

Baker, Houston. (1984). *Blues, Ideology and Afro-American Literature*. Chicago: University of Chicago Press.

Balandier, Georges. (1965). *La Vie Quotidienne au Royaume de Kongo du XVIe au XVIIIe Stécles*. Paris: HACHETTE.

Bangura, Abdul K. (2002). *Mario Fenyo on the Third World: A Reader*. San Jose: Writers' Club Press.

Bangura, Abdul K. (1994). *Research Methodology and African Studies*. Lanham, MD: University Press of America.

Barclay, Alexander. (1823). *A Practical View of the Present State of Slavery*. London: Mnemosyne Publishing Company.

Barnes, Sandra T. (1997). Africa's Ogun transformed: Introduction to the second edition. Sabdra T. Barnes, ed. *Africa's Ogun: Old World and New*. Bloomington: Indiana University Press.

Barnet, Miguel. (1968). *The Autobiography of a Runaway Slave: Esteban Montejo*. New York: Curbstone Press.

Barrett, Leonard E. (1968). *The Rastafarians,* rev. ed. New York: Beacon Press.

Bascom, William R. (1972). *Shango in the New World*. Austin, TX: University of Texas Press.

Bascom, William R. (1971). The focus on Cuban Santerìa. In Michael M. Horowitz, ed. *Peoples and Cultures of the Caribean*. Garden City, NY: The Natural History Press.

Bascom, William R. (1969). *The Yoruba of Southwestern Nigeria*. New York: Waveland Press.

Bass, L. R. 1979. The Constitution as symbol: The interpersonal sources of meaning of a secondary symbol. *American Journal of Political Science* 23,1.

Bastide, Roger. (1971). *African Civilizations in the New World*. New York: Harper and Row.

Bastide, Roger. (1970). Color, racism, and Christianity. In B. N. Schwartz and R.Disch, eds *White Racism: Its History, Pathology and Practice*. New York: Dell Publishing Co.

Bastide, Roger. (1967). *Les Ameriques Noires; les Civilisations Africaines dans le Nouveau Monde*. Paris: Bibliotheque scientifique.

Beckwith, Martha W. (1929). *Black Roadways: A Study of Jamaican Folk Life*. Chapel Hill, NC: University of North Carolina Press.

Beckwith, Martha W. (1928). *Jamaican Folklore*. New York: American Folk-lore, G.E. Stechert and Company.

Beckwith, Martha W. (1923). *Christmas Mummuins in Jamaica*. New York: Vassar College.

Berry, William. (2005). *The Mass Media and the Globalization of Racial Prejudice: Representations of Africa and Blackness in Newspapers in the Dominican Republic*. Santo Domingo: ATWS.

Bettelheim, Judith. (1976). The Jonkonnu festival. *Jamaica Journal* 10:20-27.

Birmingham-Pokorny, Elba, ed. (1995). *An English Anthology of Afro-Hispanic Writers of the Twentieth Century Cuba*. London: Zed Books.

Black, Max. (1969). *The Labyrinth of Language*. New York: The New American Library.

Blackshire-Belay, Carol Aisha, ed. (1996). *The African-German Experience: Critical Essays*. Westport, CT: Greenwood Publishing Group.

Blackstock, Sarah. (2001). Researching African-Caribbean family history. Available: http://www.birminghamblackhistory.com Retrieved: May 28, 2005.

Blainey, Geoffrey. (1968). *The Tyranny of Distance: How Distance Shaped Australia's History*. London: Macmillan.

Bolton, H. Carrington. (1890). Gombay: A festival rite of Bermuda Negroes. *Journal of American Folklore* 3:2.

Bosch, Juan. (1981). *De Cristobal Colon a Fidel Castro: El Caribe Frontera Imperial*. Havana Casa de las Americas.

Branch, T. (1988). *Parting the Waters*. New York: Simon and Schuster.

Branche, Jerome. (1999). Negrismo: Hibridez cultural, autoritarianismo, y la questión de la nación. *Revista Iberoamericana: Literatura Afro-hispanica*, special edition, 188-189.

Brathwaite, Edward Kamau. (1977). Caliban, Ariel, and Unprospero in the conflict of creolization: A study of the slave revolt in Jamaica in 1831-32. In Vera Rubin and Arthur Tuden, eds. *Comparative Perspectives on Slavery in New World Plantation Societies.* New York: New York Academy of Sciences.

Brathwaite, Edward Kamau. (Spring 1974). The African presence in Caribbean literature. *Daedalus* 103:73-109.

Brathwaite, Edward Kamau. (1974). *Contradictory Omens, Cultural Diversity and Integration in the Caribbean.* Mona, Jamaica: Savacou.

Brathwaite, Edward Kamau. (1971). *The Development of Creole Society in Jamaica, 1770-1820.* Oxford, England: Clarendon Press.

Brathwaite, Edward Kamau. (1969). *Islands.* New York: Oxford University Press.

Brathwaite, Edward Kamau. (1967). *Rites of passage.* New York: Oxford University Press.

Brizan, George. (1984). *Grenada, Island of Conflict; from Amerindians to People's Revolution, 1498-1979.* London: Zed Books.

Brooks, T. (1984). *America's Black Musical Heritage.* Englewood Cliffs, NJ: Prentice-Hall, Inc.

Brown, Beverly. (September 1926). George Liele: Black Baptist and Pan Africanist, 1750-1826. *Savacou* 11/12:58-67.

Brown, Karen McCarthy. (1997). Systematic remembering, systematic forgetting: Ogou in Haiti. In Sandra T. Barnes, ed. Africa's Ogun: Old World and New. Bloomington: Indiana University Press.

Brown, Karen McCarthy. (1984). Why women need the war god. In J. Kalven and M. Buckley. Women's Spirit Bonding. New York: Pilgrim Press.

Buchner, J. H. (1854). *The Moravians in Jamaica, History of the Mission of the United Brethrens' Church to the Negroes in the Island of Jamaica, from the Year 1754 to 1854*. London, England: Longman and Company.

Bueno, Salvador. (May-June 1976). 'La canción gel bongo': Sobre la cultural mulata de Cuba. *Cuadernos Americanos* 206:96-101.

Bynum, Edward Bruce. (1999). *The African Unconscious: Roots of Ancient Mysticism and Modern Psychology*. New York: Teachers College Press.

Cabrera, Lydia. (1970/2001). *Reframes de Negros Viejos*. Miami: Ediciones Universal.

Cabrera, Lydia. (1970/2001). *Otán Iyebiyé: las Piedras Preciosas*. Miami: Ediciones Universal.

Cabrera, Lydia. (1970/2001). *La sociedad Secreta Abakuá: Narrada por Viejos Adeptos*. Miami: Ediciones Universal.

Cabrera, Lydia. (1968/2001). *El Monte*, 2nd ed. Miami: Ediciones Universal.

Cabrera, Lydia. (1957/2001). *Abagó, Vocabulario Lucumí*. Havana: Ediciones Universal.

Carter Harrison, Paul, Victor Leo Walker III and Gus Edwards, eds. (2002). *Black Theatre; Ritual Performance in the African Diaspora*. Philadelphia: Temple University Press.

Cassidy, Frank. (1971). Jamaican Creole and Twi: Some comparisons. Paper presented at the Conference on Creole Languages and Educational Development, Trinidad.

Cassidy, Frederick G. (1970). *Dictionary of Jamaican English*. Cambridge: Cambridge University Press.

Césaire, Aimé. (1990). *Lyric and Dramatic Poetry, 1946-82*. Charlottesville, University Press of Virginia.

Césaire, Aimé. (1968). *A Season in the Congo*. Translated by Ralph Manheim. New York, Grove Press.

Césaire, Aimé. (1956). *Cahier d'un Retour au Pays Natal*. Paris: Presence Africaine.

Chanda, Tirthankar. A new lease on life for Black French-language literature. www.france.diplomatic.fr

Chinosole. (2001). *African Diaspora and Autobiographics*. New York: Peter Lang.

Cobb, R. and C. Elder. (1976). Symbolic identification and political behavior. *American Politics Quarterly* 4:305-332.

Cobley, Alan. (February 2001). African studies in the West Indies. *H-Africa Africa Forum*. Available: http://www.h-net.org/~africa/africaforum/Colby.html Retrieved: May 28, 2005.

Coe, Michael. (1977). *Mexico*. England: Thames and Hudson.

Comitas, Lambros and David Lowenthal, eds. (1973). *Slaves, Free Men, Citizens: West Indian Perspectives*. New York: Doubleday Publishing.

Commitas, Lambros and David Lowenthal. (1973). *Work and Family Life*. New York: Doubleday Publishing.

Condé, Maryse. (1992). *Tree of Life*. New York: Ballantine Books.

Condé, Maryse. (1982). *Heremakhonon*. Translated by Richard Philcox. Washington, D.C., Three Continents Press.

Conroy Kennedy, Ellen, ed. (1975). *The Negritude Poets*. New York: Thunder's Mouth Press.

Cook, Mercer. The literary contributions of the French West Indian. *Chickenbones: A Journal*.

Cook, Sherburne F. and Woodrow Borah. (1971-74). *Essays in Population History: Mexico and the Caribeban*, 2 vols. Berkeley, CA: University of California Press.

Cook, Sherburne F. and Woodrow Borah. (1968). *The Population of the Mixteca Alta*. Berkeley, CA: University of California Press.

Coulthard, G. R. (1962). *Race and Colour in Caribbean Literature*. London: Oxford University Press.

Crahan, Margaret E. and Franklin W. Knight, eds. (1979). *Africa and the Caribbean: The Legacies of a Link*. Baltimore, MD: Johns Hopkins University Press.

Crahan, Margaret E. and Franklin W. Knight. (1979). The African migration and the origins of an Afro-American society and culture. In Margaret E. Crahan and Franklin W. Knight, eds. *Africa and the Caribbean: The Legacies of a Link*. Baltimore, MD: Johns Hopkins University Press.

Craighton, Al. (n.d.). Guyana under siege: African heritage in Guyana. Available: http://www.guyanaundersiege.com/Cultural/African%20heritage%.... Retrieved: June 9, 2005.

Craton, Michael M. (1978). *Searching for the Invincible Man: Slaves and Plantation Life in Jamaica*. Cambridge, MA: Harvard University Press.

Crowley, Daniel. (1956). The midnight robbers. *Caribbean Quarterly* 4:263-74.

Cruz, Shamil. (Spring 2000). African Americans in the Caribbean and Latin America. Available: http://www.saxakali.com Retrieved: June 3, 2005.

Cundall, Frank and Izett Anderson, eds. (1927). *Jamaican Proverbs and Sayings*, 2nd ed. London: Institute of Jamaica. Reprinted in Kingston, Jamaica, 1972.

Cuny-Hare, M. (1936/1974). *Negro Musicians and Their Music*. New York: Da Capo Press.

Daku, Kwame Yeba. (1970). *Trade and Politics on the Gold Coast, 1600-1720*. Oxford: Oxford University Press.

Dalby David. (1971). Ashanti survivals in the language and traditions of the Windward Maroons of Jamaica. *African Language Studies* 12:31-51.

Dathorne, O. R. (1974). *The Black Mind: A History of African Literature*. Minneapolis, MN: University of Minnesota Press.

Dathorne, O. R. (1964). Africa in West Indian literature. *Black Orpheus* 16:42-54.

Davidson, Basil. (1970). *The Lost Cities of Africa*. England: Little Brown.

Davies, Catherine. (1997). *A Place in the Sun? Women Writers in 20th Century*. New York: St. Martin's Press.

Dawes, Neville. (1960). *The Last Enchantment*. London: Peepal Tree Press Ltd.

D'Costa, Jean and Jack Berry. (1971). Some considerations of tone in Jamaican Creole. Paper presented at the Conference on Caribbean Linguistics, Kingston, Jamaica.

de Burgos, Julia. In Thomson Gale's Hispanic heritage. www.gale.com/ free_resources/chh/io/deburgos

DeCamp, David. (1977). The development of Pidgin and Creole studies. In Albert Valdman, ed. *Symposium on Cultural Identity of French-speaking in the Americas*. Bloomington, IN: Indiana University Press.

De Costa. Miriam, ed. (1977). *Blacks in Hispanic Literature: Critical Essays*. Port Washington, NY: Kennikat Press.

de Craemer, Willy, Jan Vansina and Renée C. Fox. (October 1976). Religious movements in Central Africa: A theoretical study. *Comparative Studies in Society and History* 18:458-75.

Defries, Amelia. (1929). *The Fortunate Islands*. London, England: Cecil Palmer.

del Monte y Tejada, Antonio. (1980). *Historia de Santo Domingo*, 4 vols. Santo Domingo, Dominican Republic: Editoria Corripio.

Denevan, William M. (1976). *The native Population of the Americas in 1492.* Madison, WI: University of Wisconsin Press.

Depestre, René. (January/February 1970). Los fundamentos soicioculturales de nuestra identidad. *Casa de las Americas* 58.

Deschamps Chapeaux, Pedro. (1967). El lenguaje Abakuá. *Etnología y Folklore* 4:39-48.

Diop, Cheikh Anta. (1991). *Civilization or Barbarism.* England: Lawrence Hill.

Dominguez Miguela, Antonia. (n.d.). 'Kalahari' or the Afro-Caribbean connection: Luis Pale's Matos' tuntún de pasa y griferia and tato la carreta made a u-yurn. University of Huelva.

Drayton, Arthur. (July 1970). West Indian consciousness in West Indian verse: A historical perspective. *Journal of Commonwealth Literature* 9:66-88.

DuBois, W. E. B. (1993). *The Souls of Black Folk.* Greenwich, CN: Fawcett Publications, 1961.

Edelman, M. (1964). *The Symbolic Uses of Politics.* Urbana: The University of Illinois Press.

Elder, C. and R. Cobb. (1983). *The Political Uses of Symbols.* New York: Longman.

Fanon, Frantz. (1963). *The Wretched of the Earth.* Trans. Constance Farrington. New York: Grove Press.

Fasold, Ralph. (2003). The social construction of a 'language.' Annual Lecture of the North West Center for Linguistics, University of Manchester, United Kingdom, April 7.

Fasold, Ralph W. (1999). Ebonic need not be English. *Issue Paper Digest*. Washington, DC: Center for Applied Linguistics.

Fasold, Ralph. (1984). *The Sociolinguistics of Society*. New York: Basil Blackwell.

Fenyo, Mario D. (1997). The African mirror. *The Journal of African Communications* 2,1:36-55.

Fierce, Mildred C. (1991). *African Studies Outside the United States: Africa, Brazil, the Caribbean*. Ithaca: Cornell University, No. 7.

Fernandez de Oviedo, Gonzalo. (1959). *Historia General y Natural de las Indias*, reprinted in Madrid: Ediciones Atlas.

Filmore, C. J. (1968). The case for case. E. Bach and R. Harms, eds. *Universals in Linguistic Theory*. New York: Holt Reinhart and Winston.

Filmore, C. J. (1968). An alternative to checklist theories of meaning. Proceedings of the first annual meeting of the Berkeley Linguistic Society, University of California.

Folkes, Karl. (March 2004). Is Jamaican patois a language? Available: http://www.jamaicans.com Retrieved: May 28, 2005.

Foner, E. ed. (1976). *America's Black Past*. New York: Harper and Row, Publishers.

Forte, Janette Bulkan. (2003). Review essay: Atlas of the languages of Suriname. *The Journal of Caribeban Ameridian History and Anthropology* URL: http://www.kacike.org/ForteAtlas.pdf pps.15. Retrieved: May 28, 2005.

Fouchet, Max-Pol. (1976). *Wilfredo Lam*. New York, 188.

Frazier, E. F. (1963). *The Negro Church in America*. Boston: Beacon Press.

Frege, G. (1892/1952). On Sense and Reference. P. T. Geach and M. Black, eds. *Translations from the Philosophic Writings of Gottlob Frege*. Oxford: Blackwell.

Fromkin, Victoria, Robert Rodman and Nina M. Hyams. (2002). *Introduction to Language*. London: Heinle Group.

Fromkin, Victoria and Robert Rodman. (1998). *An Introduction to Language* 6th ed. Fort Worth, TX: Harcourt College.

Fyfe, Christopher. (1976). The dynamics of African dispersal: The Trans-Atlantic slave trade. In Martin L. Kilson and Robert I. Rotberg, eds. *The African Diaspora: Interpretive Essays*. Cambridge, MA: Harvard University Press.

Gates, Henry Louis, Jr. (1991). *The Signifying Monkey: A Theory of African-American Literary Criticism*. United States: The H.W. Wilson Company.

Gates, Henry Louis, Jr. (1988). *The Signifying Monkey: A Theory of Afro-American Literary Criticism*. New York:
Oxford University Press.

Gazdar, G. (1979). *Pragmatics: Implicature, Presupposition and Logical Form*. New York: Academic Press.

George, Nelson. (1998). *Hip Hop America*. New York: Penguin Books.

Gilroy, Paul. (1993). *The Black Atlantic: Modernity and Double Consciousness*, Cambridge: Harvard University Press.

Gilroy, Paul. (1987). *There Ain't No Black in the Union Jack: The Cultural Politics of Race and Nation*. London: Melbourne: Hutchinson. Reprint, Chicago: University of Chicago Press, 1991.

Goodwin Jr., Paul B. (2005). Studies in Latin America, 12th ed. and Population Reference Bureau. www.prb.org

Goodwin Jr., Paul B. (2003). *Global studies Latin America*, 10th ed. Guilford, CT: McGraw-Hill/Dushkin.

Grice, H. P. (1957). Meaning. *Philosophical Review* (vol. 64:377-388).

Guillén, Nicolás. (1974). *Obra Poética, 1920-1972,* 2 vols. Havana, Cuba: Loguez Ediciones.

Hall, Robert. (1958). Creolized languages and 'genetic relationships.' *Word* 14:367-73.

Hall, Stuart. (1992). What is this "Black" in Black popular culture? In Ed. by G. Dent. ed. Black Popular Culture. Seattle: Bay Press.

Hancock, Ian. (1971). A provisional comparison of the English-based Atlantic Creoles. In Dell Hymes, ed. *Pidginization and Creolizatioon of Languages.* New York: Cambridge University Press.

Harris, Wilson. (1967). *Tradition, the Writer and Society.* London: New Beacon Press.

Heine, Bernd and Derek Nurse, eds. (2000). *African Languages: An Introduction.* Cambridge: Cambridge University Press.

Henry, Paget and Paul Buhle. (1992). *C.L.R. James' Caribbean.* Durham, Duke University Press.

Herskovits, Melville J. (1941). *The Myth of the Negro Past.* New York: Harper and Row and Boston: Beacon Press.

Higman, B. W., ed. (1999). *General History of the Caribbean.* Vol. VI, ed. B. W. Higman, London: UNESCO

Hill, Errol. (1972). *The Trinidad Carnival: Mandate for a National Theater.* Austin, TX: University of Texas Press.

Hoetink, Harry. (1979). The cultural links. In Margaret E. Crahan and Franklin W. Knight, eds. *Africa and the Caribbean: The Legacies of a Link.* Baltimore, MD: Johns Hopkins University Press.

Hoffman, Léon-François. "Présentation de *Gouverneurs de la Rosée.* In *Haiti : Lettres et l'Être.* Toronto, Canada : GREF.

Holloway, J. E., ed. (1990). *Africanisms in American Culture*. Bloomington: Indiana University Press.

Holloway, J. E. and W. K. Vass. (1993). *The African Heritage of American English*. Bloomington: Indiana University Press.

Holloway, J. E. (n.d). The impact of African languages on American English. Available: http://www.sleveryinamerica.org Retrieved: May 28, 2005.

Hull, R. W. (1972). *Munyakare: African Civilization Before the Batuuree*. New York: John Wiley and Sons, Inc.

Hurault, Jean. (1970). *Africains de Guyane: La Vie Matérielle et l'art de Noirs Refugies de Guyane*. The Hague: Mouton.

Huttar, George. (1974). Some Kwa-like features of Djuka syntax. Paper presented at the Summer Institute of Linguistics, Sidney, Australia.

Hymes, Dell, ed. (1971). *Pidginization and Creolization of Languages*. New York: Cambridge University Press.

Ice-T. (1991). Straight up nigga. *Original Gangsta*, New York: sire Records.

Jamaican Government Public Relations Office. n.d. *The Jamaican Directory of Personalities*. Kingston, Jamaica: City Printery, Inc.

James, C.L.R. (1963). *The Black Jacobins: Toussaint L'Ouverture and the San Domingo Revolution*. New York: Vintage.

James, C. L. R.. (1938). *The Black Jacobins; Toussaint L'Ouverture and the San Domingo Revolution*. London: Secker and Warburg.

Jay, Paul. (1999). Hibridity, identity and cultural commerce in Claude McKay's *Banana Bottom*. *Callaloo* 22.1:176-194.

Johnson, G. B. and R. R. Campbell. (1981). *Black Migration in America*. Durham, NC: Duke University Press.

Johnson, J. W. (1925). *Book of American Negro-Spirituals.* New York: Viking Press.

Jones, E. (1964). The psychology of constitutional monarchy. E. Jones, ed. *Essays in Applied Psycho-Analysis.* London: The Hogart Press.

Journal of African Civilization. (March 16, 2006).

Judy, R. A. T. (2004). On the question of N***A authenticity. M. Forman and M. A. Neal, eds. That's the Joint!: The Hip-Hop Studies Reader. New York: Routledge.

Karttunen, L. (1973). Presuppositions of compound sentences. *Linguistic Inquiry* (vol. iv, no. 2).

Karttunen, L. (1971). Implicative verbs. *Language* (vol. 47).

Kilson, Martin and Robert Rotberg, eds. (1976). *The African Diaspora: Interpretive Essays.* Cambridge, MA: Harvard University Press.

King, Lloyd. (1972). Mr. Black in Cuba. *African Studies Association of the West Indies Bulletin* 5:25-26.

King, Nicole. (2001). *C.L.R. James and Creolization.* Jackson: University Press of Mississippi.

Kloss, Heinz. (1967). Abstand language and ausbau languages. *Anthropological Linguistics* 9:29-41.

Kloss, Heinz. (1966). Types of multilingual communities: A discussion of ten variables. *Sociological Inquiry* 36:135-145.

Knight, Franklin W., ed. (1997). *General History of the Caribbean*, Vol. 3, London: Macmillan.

Knight, Franklin W. (1978). *The Caribbean: the Genesis of a Fragmented Nationalism.* New York: Oxford University Press.

Knight, Franklin W. (1974). *The African Dimension in Latin American societies.* New York: Macmillan.

Labrador-Rodriquez, Sonia. (1999). Mulatos entreblancos: José Celso Barbsa y Antonio S. Pedreira. *Revista Iberoamericana* 713-731.

Lamming, George. (1981). *Of Age and Innocence.* London: Allison & Busby.

Lamming, George. (September/October 1969). Actitudes de la literatura antillana con respecto a Africa. *Casa de las Americas* 56:120-25.

Lamming, George. (Spring 1966). Caribeban literature: The black rock of Africa. *African Forum* 1:32-52.

Lamming, George. (1953). *In the Castle of My Skin.* Boston: McGraw Hill.

Laroche, Maximillen. (1976). The myth of the Zombie. In Roland Smith, ed. *Exile and Tradition: Studies in African and Caribbean Literature.* Halifax, Nova Scotia: Holmes and Meir Publishers.

Larrazabal Blanco, Carlos. (1967). *Los Negros y la Esclavitud en Santo Domingo.* Santo Domingo: Amigo del Hogar.

Las Casas, Bartolomé. (1951). *Historia de las Indias.* Reprinted in 3 vols., Mexico: Fondo de la Cultura.

Lasswell, H. (1965). *World Politics and Personal Insecurity.* New York: The Free Press.

Lattany, Kristin Hunter. (1993). "Off-timing": Stepping to the different Drummer. In Gerald Early, ed. Lure and Loathing: Essays on Race, Identity, and the Ambivalence of Assimilation. New York: Penguin Books.

Lawton, David. (1971). Tone and Jamaican Creole. Paper presented to the Conference on Caribbean Linguistics, Kingston, Jamaica.

Lewis, Gordon K. (1968). *Growth of the Modern West Indies.* New York: Monthy Review Press.

Lewis, Gordon K. (1983). *Main Currents in Caribbean Thought: The Historical Evolution of Caribbean Society in Its Ideological Aspects, 1492-1900*. Baltimore, MD: Johns Hopkins University Press.

Lewis, Maureen Warner. (1979). The African impact on language and literature in the English-speaking Caribbean. In Margaret E. Crahan and Franklin W. Knight, eds. *Africa and the Caribbean: The Legacies of a Link*. Baltimore, MD: Johns Hopkins University Press.

Lherisson, Lanah. (May 2000). Creole language in Haiti. Available: http://www.saxakali.com Retrieved: May 28, 2005.

Linsley, Robert. (2002). Wilfredo Lam: Painter of Negritude. In K. N. Parinder, ed. Race-ing Art History: Critical Readoings in Race and Art History. New York: Routledge.

Lisembé, Elebé. (1973). *Chant de la Terre/Chant de l'Eau*, Paris: Pierre Oswald.

Levinson, S. (1983). *Pragmatics*. Cambridge: Cambridge University Press.

Livingston, James T. (1974). *Caribbean Rhythms: The Emerging English Literature of the West Indies*. New York: Washington Square Press.

Long, Charles. (1986). *Significations: Signs, Symbols, and Images in the Interpretation of Religion*. Philadelphia:
Fortress Press.

Lovelace, Earl. (1998). *Salt*. New York: Persea Books.

Lyons, J. (1977). *Semantics*. Cambridge: Cambridge University Press.

MacDonald, John S. and Leatrice D. MacDonald. (1973). Transformation of African and Indian family traditions in the South Caribbean. *Comparative Studies in Society and History* 15:171-98.

Maran, Robert. (1921/1988). *Batouala*. London: Heinemann.

Marquez, Robert. (1974). *Latin American Revolutionary Poetry*. New York: Monthly Review Press.

Marzan, Julio. (1995). The poetry and antipoetry of Luis Pales Matos. *Callaloo*, 18, 2:506-523.

Mathurin. Lucille. (n.d). *The Rebel Woman in the British West Indies during Slavery*. Kingston, Jamaica: African-Caribbean Publications.

Mazrui, A. A. (1977). *Africa's International Relations*. Boulder, Colorado: Westview Press.

McHardy, Cecile. (May 2000). Gulah culture. Available: http://www.edu-cyberg.com Retrieved: May 28, 2005.

McKay, Claude. (1933/2005). *Banana Bottom*. Washington, D.C.: Xpress.

McLaughlin, E. C. (December 1932). Gombeys and casava pie. *The Bermudian* 1.

Meli, F. (1988). *A History of the ANC: South Africa Belongs to Us*. Harare: Zimbabwe Publishing House.

Mellafe, Rolando. (1959). *La Introducción de la Esclavitud Negra en Chile: Tráfico y Rutas*. Santiago, Chile: Editorial Universitaria.

Merelman, R.(1966). Learning and legitimacy. *American Political Science Review* 60:553-561.

Metraux, Alfred. (1972). *Voodoo in Haiti*. New York: Schocken Books.

Mintz, Sidney W. and Richard Price. (1976). *An Anthropological Approach to the Afro-American Past: A Caribbean Perspective* (Occasional Papers in Social Change). Philadelphia, PA: Institute for the Study of Human Issues.

Morales Carrion, Arturo (1952). *Puerto Rico and the Non-Hispanic Caribbean*. Rio Piedras: University of Puerto Rico Press.

Morejón, Nancy. (1979). *Parajes de ana Época*. Havana, Cuba: Editorial Letras Caubanas.

Moreno Fraginals, Manuel, ed. (1977a). *Africa en América Latina*. Mexico City: Siglo Veintiuno Editores.

Moreno Fraginals, Manuel. (1977b). Africa in Cuba: A quantitative analysis of the African population in the Island of Cuba. In Vera Rubin and Arthur Tuden, eds. *Comparative Perspectives on Slavery in New World Plantation Societies*. New York: New York Academy of Sciences.

Naipaul, V. S. (2002). *Miguel Street*. New York: Vintage.

Nesbitt, Nick. (2002). Negritude. www.geocities.com/africanwriters

Ntonfo, André. (1997). *Le Roman Indigéniste Haitien: Esthétique et Idéologie*. New Orleans: University Press of the South.

Nuñez, Elisabeth. Maryse Condé, grande dame of Caribbean Literature. www.unesco.org/courier

Ola Oke, David. (March 1977). On the genesis of New World Black English. *Caribbean Quarterly* 23:61-79.

Olliz Boyd, Antonio. (1977). The concept of Black awareness as a thematic approach in Latin American literature. In Miriam De Costa, ed. *Blacks in Hispanic Literature: Critical Essays*. Port Washington, NY: Kennikat Press.

Olmsted, David. (1953). Comparative notes on Yoruba and Lacumi. *Languages* 29:157-64.

Ortiz, Fernando. (1917). *Hampa Afro-Cubana: Los Negros Brujos* (apuntes para un estudio de etnología). Madrid: Editorial America.

Ortiz, Fernando. (1906). *Hampa Afro-Cubana: Los Negros Esclavos*. Havana: Revista Bimestre Cubana.

Palmer, Colin A. (1976). *Slaves of the White God: Blacks in Mexico, 1570-1650.* Cambridge, MA: Harvard University Press.

Parrinder, G. (1969). *Religion in Africa.* London: Penguin Books.

Parry, J. H. and P. M. Sherlock. (1956). *A Short History of the West Indies.* London: Macmillan, 1ˢᵗ ed.

Patterson, Orlando. (1967). *The Sociology of Slavery: an Analysis of the Origins, Development, and Structure of Negro Slave Society in Jamaica.* London: McGibbon and Fee.

Perkins, William Eric. (1996). The rap attack: An introduction. In W. Perkins, ed. *Droppin' Science: Critical Essays on Rap Music and Hip-Hop Culture.* Philadelphia, PA: Temple University Press.

Perkinson, James. (2005). *Shamanism, Racism, and Hip-Hop Culture: Essays on White Supremacy and Black Subversion.* New York: Palgrave Macmillan Press.

Perkinson, James. (2001). Ogu's iron or Jesus' irony: Who's zooming who in Diasporic possession cult activity? *Journal of Religion* 81, 4:566-594.

Perry, Imani. (200). *Prophets of the Hood: Politics and Poetics in Hip Hop.* Durham, NC: Duke University Press.

Phaf, Ineke. (1999). El 'Cuaderno' de Nancy Morejón. *Revista Iberoamericana* 537.

Price, Richard. (1973). Kikongo and Saramaccan: A reappraisal. *Journal of African Languages* 12.

Price, Richard, ed. (1973). *Maroon Societies: Rebel Slave Communities in the Americas.* Garden City, NY: Anchor Books.

Price, Richard. (1966). Caribbean fishing and fishermen: A historical sketch. *American Anthropologist* 68:1363-84.

Price, Richard and Sally Price. (1972). Saramaka onomastics: An Afro-American naming system. *Ethnology* 11:341-67.

Quarles, B. (1964). *The Negro in the Making of America* (rev ed). New York: Cotier Macmillan Publishers.

Ramsaran, Ramesh, ed. (2002). *Caribbean Survival and the Global Challenge.* Kingston: Ian Randle.

Rivera Casellas, Zaira O. (1999). Cuerpo y raza: el ciclo de la identidad en la literaturą puertorriqueña. *Revista Iberoamericana* 633-647.

Roberts, John Storm. (1974). *Black Music of Two Worlds.* New York: Praeger.

Rochefort, Charles de. (1658). *Histoire Naturelle et Morale des Antilles de l'Amerique ...* Rotterdam: Reinier Leers.

Rodney, Walter. (1981). *A History of the Guyanese Working People, 1881-1905.* London: Heinemann.

Rose, Tricia. (1994). *Black Noise: Rap Music and Black Culture in Contemporary America.* Hanover, NH: Wesleyan University Press: Published by University Press of New England.

Roumain, Jacques. (1944) *Gouverneurs de la rosée.* In *Haiti : Letres et l'Être.* Toronto, Canada : GREF.

Russell, B. (1905). On denoting. *Mind* 14:479-493.

Russell, B. (1957). Mr. Strawson on referring. *Mind* 66:385-389.

Saco, José Antonio. (1938). *Historia de las esclavitud de la Raza Africana en el Mundo Nuevo y en Especial en los Paises Américo-Hispanos.* Havana, Cuba: Cultural.

Salkey, Andrew. (1973). *Anancy's Score.* London: Bogle-L'Ouverture Press Ltd.

Schomburgk, R. H. (1971). *The History of Barbados*. London: Frank Cass (1st ed. 1848).

Selvon, Samuel. (1957). *Ways of Sunlight*. Trinidad/China: Longman.

Selvon, Samuel. (1952). *A Brighter Sun*. Longman.

Senior, Olive. (1983). *A-Z of Jamaican Heritage*. Kingston, Jamaica: Heinemann Educational Books (Caribbean) Limited and The Gleaner Company Limited.

Sherwood, Marika. (2006). *Multi-ethnic History*. England: unknown.

Simpson, George Eaton. (December 1962). The Shango cult in Nigeria and Trinidad. *American Anthropologist* 64:1204-19.

Singham, A. W. and N. L. Singham. (1976). Jamaica. *The World Book* Encyclopedia, vol. 11:J-K. Chicago: Field Enterprises Educational Corporation.

Smith, Jeremy. (1996). *Historical Study of English: A Dynamic Approach*. New York: Routeledge.

Smith, M. G. (1960). The African heritage in the Caribbean. In Vera Rubin, ed. *Caribbean Studies: A Symposium*. Seattle, WA: University of Washington Press.

Spencer, J. M. (1990). *Protest and Praise: Sacred Music of Black Religion*. Minneapolis: Portress Press.

Stalnaker, R. C. (1974). Pragmatic presuppositions. M. K. Munitz and P. K. Unger, eds. *Semantics and Philosophy*. New York: New York University Press.

Stalnaker, R. C. (1978). Assertion. In P. Cole, ed. *Syntax and Semantics 9: Pragmatics*. New York: Academic Press.

Stiffler, Steve and Mark Moberg, eds. (2003). *Banana Wars: Power, Production and History in the Americas*. Durham: Duke University Press.

Stinchcomb, Dawn. (March 8-21, 2004). Literary heritage. www.las.iastate.edu/newnews/stitchcomb

Stinchcomb, Dawn. (2004). *The Development of Literary Blackness in the Dominican Republic*. Gainesville, FL: University Press of Florida.

Strawson, P. (1950). On referring. *Mind* 59:320-344.

Strawson, P. (1952). *Introduction to Logical Theory*. London: Metheun.

Taylor, A. (1976). *Travail and Triumph*. Westport, CT: Greenwood Press.

Taylor, Douglas N. (1963). The origin of West Indian Creole languages in evidence from grammatical categories. *American Anthropologist* 65:800-14.

Taylor, J. E. (1975). Something on my mind: A cultural and historical interpretation of spiritual texts. *Ethnomusicology* xix, 3.

Tax, Sol. ed. (1967). *Acculturation in the Americas*. New York: Cooper Square Publishers.

Thompson, Robert Farris. (1996). Hip Hop 101. In W. Perkins, ed. *Droppin' Science: Critical Essays on rap Music and Hip Hop Culture*. Philadelphia: Temple University Press.

Thompson, Robert Farris. (1983). *Flash of the Spirit: African and Afro-American Art and Philosophy*. New York:
Vintage Books.

Thompson, Robert W. (1961). A note on some possible affinities between the Creole dialects of the Old World and those of the New. *Creole Language Studies* 2:107-13.

Thompson, Vincent Bakpetu. (1988). *The Making of the African Diaspora in the Americas 1441-1900*. Harlow: Longman.

Thompson, Vincent Bakpetu. (1987). *The Making of the African Diaspora in the Americas 1441-1900*, Burnt Mill, UK: Longman.

Tillis, Antonio. (2003). Awakening the Caribbean African: the socio-political poetry of Blas Jimenez. *Afro-Hispanic Review* 22, 2:29-38

Todaro, Michael. (1997). *Economic Development in the Third World*. New York: Longman House.

Toute la poésie. (2005). www.toutelapoesie.com/poemes/césaire

Trudgill, Peter.(2001). *Sociolinguistics: An Introduction to Language and Society* 4th ed. New York: Penguin Group.

Trudgill, Peter. (1974). *Sociolinguistics*. New York: Penguin Books.

Trudgill, Peter and Lars-Gunnar Andersson. (1992). *Bad Language*. New York: Penguin Group.

Twiggs, Robert D. (1973). *Pan-African Language in the Western Hemisphere: A Redefinition of Black Dialect as a Language and the Culture of the Black Dialect*. North Quincy, MA: Christopher.

Van Sertima, Ivan. (1976). *They Came Before Columbus-The African Presence in the Ancient America*. Washington, DC: Random House.

Vlahos, O. (1967). *African Beginnings*. Greenwich, Connecticut: Fawcett Publications, Inc.

Walker, D. (1892/1965). Appeal to the coloured citizens of the world. In Herbert Aptheker, ed. *One Continual Cry: David Walker's Appeal to the Coloured Citizens of the World (1929-1930), Its Setting and Its Meaning*. New York: Humanities Press.

Walker, Sheila. (1972). *Ceremonial Spirit Possession in Africa and Afro-America: Forms, Meanings, and Functional Significance for Individuals and Social Groups*. Leiden: E.J. Brill.

Warner-Lewis, Maureen. (n.d). *Review of John Stevenson's Trinidad Yoruba—From Mother Tongue to Memory* (University of Alabama Press, 1996). Available: http:inaccs.com.bb Retrieved: June 4, 2005.

Warner-Lewis, Maureen. (1973). Odomankoma 'kyerema se ... *Caribbean Quarterly* 19:51-99.

White, Hayden. (1978). *Tropics of Discourse: Essays in Cultural Criticism.* Baltimore: Johns Hopkins University Press.

Williams, Daniel. (2005). In France, anthems of alienation. *The Washington Post* (Nov. 24), A29.

Williams, Eric. (1970). *From Columbus to Castro: The History of the Caribbean.* London: Andre Deutsch.

Williams, Eric. (1964). *Capitalism and Slavery.* London: Andre Deutsch.

Williams, Eric. (1962). *History of the People of Trinidad and Tobago.* Port of Spain: PNM Publishing.

Williams, Lorna V. (1979). The African presence in the poetry of Nicolás Gullén. In Margaret E. Crahan and Franklin W. Knight, eds. *Africa and the Caribbean: The Legacies of a Link.* Baltimore, MD: Johns Hopkins University Press.

Witvliet, T. (1987). *The Way of the Black Messiah.* Oak Park, IL: Meyer, Stone, and Company, Inc.

Web Sites

http://213.131.178.162
http://bleaseswebworld.com
http://community-2.webtv.net
http://debate.uvm.edu
http://grenada.caribbeanway.com
http://fotw.vexillum.com
http://encarta.msn.com
http://en.webcaraibes.com
http://en.wikipedia.org
http://husky1.stmaeys.ca
http://language.school-explorer.com
http://mason.gmu.edu

http://news.bbc.co.uk
http://roughguides.iexplore.com
http://webcenter.travel.aol.com
http://world-flags.info
http://www.alertnet.org
http://www.bahamas.com
http://www.britanica.com
http://www.cubanet.org
http://www.divisionofculture.org
http://www.gotopuertorico.com
http://www.guyana.org
http:www.guyanaundersiege.com
http://www.lennoxhonychurch.com
http://www.st-maarten.com
http://www.wil.org
http://www.sintmaarte,net
http://www.seinebight.com
http://www.tlfq.ulaval.ca
http://www.nbportal.com
http://www.afrocubaweb.com
http://www.afropop.org
http://www.answers.com
http://www.absoluteastronomy.com
http://www.belizeans.com
http://www.southernbelize.com
http://www.bonbini.com
http://www.bu.edu
http://www.caribbeanchoice.com
http://www.nationmaster.com
http://www.skyviews.com
http://www.papiamedia.com
http://www.geographia.com
http://www.companylink.co.za
http://www.experiencebermuda.com
http://www.courses.vcu.edu
http://www.infobonaire.com
http://www.lafi.org
http://www.sabatourism.com

http://www.faqs.org
http://www.virginesles.com
http://lonelyplanet.com
http://www.edu-cyberpg.com
http://www.fodors.com
http://www.rosetaproject.org
http://www.welcometothecaribbean.com
http://www.timespub.tc
http://www.dtmag.com
http://www.savory-co.com
http://www.state.gov
http://www.otrabandarecords.com
http://www.sbgmusic.com
http://www-user.tu-chemnitz.de
http://www.savethechildren.org
http://www.neworleansmistic.com
http://www.indiana.edu
http://www.ingentaconnect.com
http:www.scholars.nus.edu
http://www.webster.edu
http://www.tiscali.co.uk
http://www.madurotravel.com
http://www.whitingbirch.co.uk
http://www2.unesco.org
http://www.lehman.cuny.edu/ile.en.ile/paroles/maran

About the Authors

Ivor Agyeman-Duah is founder of the Centre for Intellectual Renewal, a public policy organization that deals with issues of culture, communication and economic development. He also serves as an advisor to The Andrew Mellon Foundation, New York on its Itaka-Aluka cultural project. As a scholar, he has been Visiting-Scholar-in-Residence at the College of Arts and Letters, the California State University, Pomona (2003) and the League of Women Voters Visiting Scholar at the University of Nebraska, Omaha (2003). Among his published works are two editions of a biography of President J.A. Kufuor of Ghana—*Between Faith and History* (2003, 2006) and *Some African Voices of Time* (1992). He currently serves as advisor on culture and communication at the Ghana High Commission in London.

Abdul Karim Bangura is a professor of International Relations and a researcher-in-residence at the Center for Global Peace in the School of International Service at American University in Washington, DC. Bangura holds a PhD in Political Science, a PhD in Development Economics, a PhD in Linguistics, and a PhD in Computer Science. He is the author of 53 books and more than 400 scholarly essays. He is the recipient of many teaching and other scholarly and service awards. He also is fluent in about a dozen African and six European languages and now studying intensively to increase his proficiency in Arabic and Hebrew.

Mario D. Fenyo is professor of History at Bowie State University of the University system of Maryland. Educated in Switzerland, France and the United States, Mario D. Fenyo has taught history and other social sciences across much of the globe—in Africa (Sudan and Nigeria), Asia, the Caribbean and Europe, not to mention the United States. He has a PhD in History. He is the author and translator of 20 other books and more than 50 scholarly articles. At the present he is "on loan" from Bowie State University to the University of Debrecen in Hungary. He strives for an ontological (as distinct from "global") and teleological understanding of our predicament and prospects in this expanding universe.

Jim Perkinson is a long-time activist and educator from inner city Detroit, currently on leave from his position as Associate Professor of Social Ethics at the Ecumenical Theological Seminary to teach in the humanities at the University of Denver. He holds a PhD in Theology/History of Religions from the University of Chicago, is the author of *White Theology: Outing Supremacy in Modernity and Shamanism, Racism, and Hip-Hop Culture: Essays on White Supremacy and Black Subversion*, and has written extensively in both academic and popular journals on questions of race, class and colonialism in connection with religion and urban culture. He is in demand as a speaker on a wide variety of topics related to his interests and a recognized artist on the spoken-word poetry scene in the inner city.

978-0-595-45193-7
0-595-45193-4

www.ingramcontent.com/pod-product-compliance
Lightning Source LLC
Chambersburg PA
CBHW020423290526
45785CB00002B/701